Fannie Blaine Elliott

Fannie Blaine Elliott

✦

Elliott Family History
1816–2003

BY EARL S. ELLIOTT, JR.
a grandson of Nathan Saunders
Elliott and Ardellia Redmon Elliott
and
great-great-grandson of
John and Frances Blaine Elliott
based on information gathered at
ELLIOTT FAMILY REUNIONS
St. Joseph, MO

iUniverse, Inc.
New York Lincoln Shanghai

Fannie Blaine Elliott
Elliott Family History 1816–2003

iUniverse, Inc.

For information address:
iUniverse, Inc.
2021 Pine Lake Road, Suite 100
Lincoln, NE 68512
www.iuniverse.com

The material in this book reflects the perspective of a scholar who has researched the civil war and the family history for nearly twenty-five years.

ISBN: 0-595-30584-9

Printed in the United States of America

This work is dedicated to Fannie Blaine Elliott and her descendents, a strong proud family of immigrants who came, saw and settled. This family line has stretched from coast to coast and continues to spread around the globe.

—F.A.Nicklow-Elliott

Contents

Contributors

Earl Saunders Elliott, Jr., Ed.D.
Charles Earl Elliott, Ph. D., son of Earl Saunders Elliott, Jr.
Florence Arlene Nicklow-Elliott, M. Ed., wife of Charles

Members of the family line include: Blaine, Boyd, Chamberlin, Carlton, Crow, Elliott, Finlay, Isgrigg and Redmon family lines. Over 3600 names are listed in our web page:

http://homepages.rootsweb.com/~eelliott/WC_TOC.HTM#CNTC

Historically, each even-numbered year in mid-June, Elliott descendants have gathered near St. Joseph, Missouri to share information, renew friendships and discuss family history. In 2002 a vote was taken to change that and make it a yearly event.

Special thanks to Harold Elliott, Janet Elliott Ewart, Carl and
Shirley Miller, Ed Richter, Melvin and Elaine Elliott, Arlan Heiser, Donna Redmon Lawson, R. Carlton, Maxine Kopp and Scott Wardlow.

Acknowledgments

Thanks to all who have shared information, communicated and worked together to compile the data. Special thanks to my daughter-in-law, Florence Arlene Nicklow-Elliott and my son, Charles Earl Elliott for their help with the formatting and editing of the book. Also, to my wife, Virginia Shrake Elliott for her support and assistance with travel, research and communications.

During the 1990's, family reunions around St. Joseph, Missouri, provided opportunity to hear stories about the Elliott clan and their travels and settlements. Cousins Harold Elliott, Janet Elliott Ewart, Virginia Shipman Stevens and Carl Miller were storytellers who brought these memories to life.

Additionally, the Public Library in Coshocton, Ohio and the Roscoe Village Foundation across the Muskingum River, provided local historical information about the Elliott family. Historian Emily Hunt provided us with Boyd and Elliott family correspondence, which gave us a clearer view of Fannie Blaine Elliott.

Ruth M. Norton, great granddaughter of George Elliott and historian at Roscoe Village, in a letter to Earl S. Elliott Jr., reported finding several old letters (June 16th 1842) written by Samuel Elliott to his brother-in-law, Daniel Boyd (Athens County)., James Elliott to his brother-in-law, Daniel Boyd (Athens County)., Maryann Boyd to her mother and father, Jane Elliott Boyd & Daniel Boyd (Athens County)., Daniel Boyd (Athens County) to Nathan Elliott (53rd OVI) about the politics of the War, written near the end of the Civil War, 1865. Roscoe Village Foundation.

Foreword

As in the words of the Irish Rovers in their song,
"Years May Come, Years May Go":
"Let's take a look behind
And see what we can find.
Last year has gone for everyone
Passed with time.
What happened to us then
Can't happen once again
And what's now all to me?
History…"

For generations, our ancestors have reflected upon what has gone before their time and on what was to come, each generation sharing what it could of what it made, what it earned and what it learned with the following new blood that was part of them. For generations, the Elliott clan has pioneered and met their circumstances. This is the story of many who bravely moved forward into unknown territory to become more and to leave more behind as a legacy of a love of adventure, a determination to proceed and persevere that serves the Elliott descendents to this day. Add to that the Irish love of laughter and you've got the Elliott clan…as strong, capable and vision-filled today as ever!

—**Florence Arlene Nicklow-Elliott**

We are searching for early connections between descendants of several BLAINE sisters. The oldest was Isabella (1750–?), then Alice (1760–?), Frances (1764–1845) and another unknown sister(1760–?). Each married Elliott, Boyd, or Finley men in Ireland. They came to America and brought their children as the new nation emerged around the turn of the 18th century. Protestant families kept family Bibles and recorded their own birth, marriage and death information. Records of Irish protestant families, especially Methodists, were poorly recorded. The official recorders of vital statistics were the Church of England and the Roman Catholic Church. Methodists were considered a radical and rebellious group. These Methodists often refused to provide the official church with any information. Such records were used for tax collection, property identification (wives and children), and military recruitment. The government informally encouraged them to leave Ireland by providing shipping tickets for widows with large families of young children, and facilitating land sales in the Colonies.

The older daughter, Isabella Blaine, married the original George Elliott in Ireland. War in Europe and conscription of Irish young men for the British army and navy was a common event. To escape, families turned to the land across the ocean. The American Colonies offered political and religious freedom as well as land with opportunity to grow. Apparently, Isabella settled in the new lands in Pennsylvania or Northwest Territory, but no one is exactly clear where they settled. One of Isabella's sons, Aaron, served in the War of 1812 with a Va. Co. (West Virginia). Eventually, Aaron lived in Rose Twp. of Carroll Co., near Holmes Co., Ohio where her younger sister, Frances "Fanny" and her family lived. "Fanny" Blaine Elliott brought several (James, Moses, Simon, Andrew, Charles, John, George, Samuel, Anne, Jane, Thomas, and Simon) of her children from Donegal, Ireland to Ohio in 1816. Fanny held 200 acres and son George held 100 acres in the same township on Doughty Creek. This land was then located in Coshocton County and would be until 1824 when a new county was formed in the north, Holmes County. While living here, Fanny's daughter Jane married Daniel Boyd in 1825, who was living with his father, Robert east of Keene. Fanny's son, Andrew (1790–1863) stayed near Doughty Creek when Fanny moved the few miles south with her son George (1798–1875) into what became Mill Creek Township of Coshocton Co., Ohio.

Basis for Sugar Creek Reunions

After the Civil War, two sons of Thomas (1807–1975), Nathan (1841–1912) and Thomas (1842–1899) moved west to Illinois where both married local women. Thomas stayed in Dawson, IL to marry Sarah Dawson. Nathan moved west to Rushville, Missouri with his wife, Martha Yates (1845–1881), and two children, Ira (1869–1953) and Lillie (1871–1941). After Martha's death in 1881, Nathan married "Arda" Redmon (1863–1916) and added 5 more children to their family line, Earl (1887–1944), Ben (1891–1944), Charles (1896–1951), Grace (1898–1961) and Ruth (1895–1975). Their children compose a group of cousins who keep in touch and hold family reunions on an irregular basis through the 1990's. They plan and hold bi-yearly reunions in mid-June during the even number years.

In some years, over 100 cousins attend the reunion held at the home of Carl Miller and later at Sugar Creek Church near Rushville, a few miles south of St. Joseph, Missouri. Perhaps, somewhere in Pennsylvania, Ohio, Indiana, Illinois, Iowa, Missouri or another state as far away as Washington, another distant cousin is searching for Elliott family roots.

The Story Begins...

In 1816, Frances Blaine Elliott (1764–1845) arrived in America from Ireland with eight of her thirteen children to settle in Coshocton County, Ohio. Her other sons and their families arrived in 1819.

In the summer of 1941, Blanche Elliott (1890–1960), 1136 Orchard Street, Coshocton, Ohio, entered the Ohioana Library Essay Contest. She received Honorable Mention, placing 6th in a field of 90 essays. Her essay began with a poem she wrote about Frances Blaine Elliott (1764–1845) and continued with seventeen pages of family information.

Beginning in the 1950's, Janet Elliott Ewart developed an interest in family genealogy. She began collecting family records, talking with older family members and became an oral historian with the records to back her up. Over 40 years, she shared, gathered and talked about Elliott, Redmon, Isgrigg, and Saunders connections with detail and accuracy. Another cousin, Harold Elliott kept in touch with his brothers and sisters over the years sharing family stories and recollections about uncles, aunts, grandparents and cousins. He tells a story in a way that captures your interest. Cousin Carl Miller talks about family with personal knowledge of St. Joseph, Missouri and the surrounding area. He encouraged family reunions with some twenty-five first cousins over the years hosting and building contacts with those who lived "out of town". Cousin Virginia Shipman Stevens kept her mother's "stuff" and shared her knowledge of family with her cousins.

During the 1960's, J. Lell Elliott (1908–1993), Professor of Chemistry at the University of Texas, Pan American 1935–1989, used summer vacations to visit Elliott sites in Coshocton County, Ohio and talk with descendants of George Elliott (1798–1875) including Zelma Wheatcraft (1914–1991). Lell traced the James Elliott (1782–1849) family line with detail and accuracy. His nephew, Melvin D. Elliott shared his family information bringing several lines of descendants together including James (1798–1875), Moses (1784–1854), George (1798–1875) and Thomas (1807–1875?).

In the 1990's, Earl Elliott, Jr. used computer technology to record and organize the work of these many cousins. Earl Jr. visited Iowa Wesleyan College to copy a photo of Charles Elliott taken when Dr Elliott was president of the College. H. Arlan Heiser arrived a few days later in Pleasant Hill, Iowa and found that Earl, Jr. had signed the visitor page with a notation seeking information about Elliott/Blaine/Boyd family. Arlan contacted Earl, Jr. and shared his knowledge and collection of Elliott family history. He wanted to learn more about his Elliott/Blaine family connections in Pennsylvania, Ohio and Ireland.

The search continues......

Melvin and Elaine Elliott placed Elliott/Blaine information in the Family History section of their local public library. A distant cousin who was searching for Andrew Elliott and Fanny Blaine contacts came across their information within a week. She called Melvin and Elaine to find out more about descendants of John and Fanny's thirteen children. In fact, she suggested contacting E. P. Kintner whose ancestors were connected to the Elliott/Blaine line through Mary (Marie) Elliott, her daughter.

Blaine/Boyd/Elliott/Finlay Early Family Connections

What happened to some of their early descendants?

Brief Chronology of the Family

1730— Moses Blaine born in Ireland?

1750— Moses Blaine (1730–?) married Jane McKee children: Isabella, Alice, Frances

1770— Isabella Blaine (1750–?) married George Elliott (1750–1799) children: Andrew W., Patrick, James, John, Mathew, Simon, Alice, Aaron

1775— Alice Blaine (1760–?) married George Finlay (1755–?) children: John, Moses, David, Catherine, Prudence,Ellinore, Isabel, Elizabeth

1781— Frances "Fanny" Blaine (May 1, 1764–Mar 28,1845) married John Elliott (1759–Mar 16,1809) on Aug. 25, 1781 in Ardara, Donegal, IR children: James, Moses, John, Mary, Simon, Andrew, Charles, John (Deacon), George, Samuel, Anne, Jane, Nancy, Thomas, Simon

1785— Ship Faithful Steward is lost near mouth of the Delaware river with few survivors, reportedly five Elliott family members perished and two survived

1792— George & Isabella Elliott arrive In WesternPennsylvania/Ohio.

1800— Fanny's son, James (Aug. 21, 1782–Sep 7, 1849) married Mary Hester Stevenson (1780–May 13, 1868) in Donegal Ireland. children: Moses, John Nesbett, Frances, James Jr., Ann Jane, Eliza, Hester. Thomas, George Nesbett, and Moses (2nd) born in Ohio.

1807— Fanny's son, Thomas Elliott born Aug. 7, Ardara, Killybegs, IR

1808— Fanny's son, Simon Elliott died at the age of 10.

3

1809— Fanny's husband, John Elliott (1759–1809), died March 16 and was buried along with two infant children in the Lower Methodist Cemetery in Killybegs, Donegal, Ireland. Their youngest son, Simon Elliott (2nd), was born Oct. 25, in Donegal.

1813— Fanny's son, Charles Elliott was licensed to preach as a member of the Irish Wesleyan Society.

1814— Charles Elliott came to America and settled in Ohio/Pennsylvania.

1815— Fanny's son, Moses Elliott (Feb. 1, 1784–1854) married Jane Cuscaden (1785–?) in Donegal, IR. children: John, James and five daughters.

1816— Frances "Fanny" Blaine Elliott and 8 of her children arrived in Baltimore Inner Harbor, purchased a wagon and traveled west on what became the National Road to Coshocton County, Ohio during the year without summer.

1818— Charles Elliott admitted to the Ohio Annual Conference of the M.E. Church and assigned to the Zanesville Circuit. George Finley and Alice Blaine with their family emigrated to Bloomfield, near where the Elliotts settled earlier.

1819— James, Moses, and Andrew arrived in Pennsylvania/Ohio. Mary stayed behind to marry James McKee, but their daughter Isabella came to Ohio later. Moses stopped in southwest Pennsylvania, then moved to settle near Carthage, Ohio in 1823.

1822— Charles Elliott spent a year as a missionary to the Wyandotte Indian Nation at Upper Sandusky. He married Phebe Leech (1802–1882) May 14 in Salem, Mercer Co., PA.children: Phebe Leech, Simon Charles, Sarah F., Fannie B., Mary Jane.

1823— daughter, Anne Elliott (May 17, 1802–Aug 16, 1825) married Lyman Shaffer. She died in childbirth, leaving an infant child.

1825— son, Samuel Elliott (May 8, 1800–1870) married Sarah Seward (Nov. 17,1804–Aug 8, 1891) in Clark Twp, Coshocton Co, OH. children: Eleanor, Simon, Phobe Jane, Eliseward, John Blaine, Albert, Nancy, Sarah, Samuel Wesley, Hester Ann.

1825— daughter, Jane Elliott (Apr. 8, 1803–Oct. 4, 1886) married Daniel Boyd (Sep. 7,1794–Aug 20, 1867) at home on Doughty Creek. children: John Elliott, Mary Ann, Jane, Kathryn, Hugh, Lucy A., William Fletcher, Fanny Blaine, Margaret. They moved to a farm near Coolville, Athens county, OH after living a few years near Keene, Coshocton, OH.

1826— son, George Elliott (Aug. 22,1798–Feb 20, 1875) married his distant cousin, Mary Elliott (Oct. 20, 1807–Aug 27, 1854), a daughter of Andrew W. Elliott (1772–1843) whose mother was Isabella Blaine Elliott, in Holmes County on Feb. 23 with Andrew Doherty officiating. children: Elizabeth Caroline, Jane, Charles, Alice, James Blaine, Andrew C., John Thomas, Samuel, Ann Jane, Fanny, Clark, George, Laura A., Catherine, Mary.

1832— son, Thomas (Aug. 6, 1807–1879?) married Lucy W. Saunders (1812–May 18, 1842) in Holmes County, OH. children: Simon, Daniel Gross, Newton, Nathan Saunders, Thomas

1834— cousin, George Finley came to Millcreek township and built himself a hewed log house on the lot directly back of the Grade School

1841— grandson, Nathan Saunders Elliott was born Feb. 1, 1841.

1841— son, Simon Elliott (Oct. 25, 1809–Sep 24, 1849) married Christiani Groff (1810–?) June 8 in Wellsville, OH. He had attended Madison College in Uniontown, PA supervised by his brother Charles.

1842— Thomas' wife, Lucy W. Saunders Elliott died May 18 at the home of Samuel Elliott after a long illness. She had another boy, Thomas, Mar 25. The funeral was a large and teary one. Both, James and Samuel wrote letters to Jane and Daniel Boyd describing the event.

1845— Frances Blaine Elliott (1764–1845) died at George's home in Mill Creek. She was buried in the Lower Methodist Cemetery in Keene, Coshocton County, Ohio.

Three Generations of John and Fanny Blaine Elliott Descendants

(1) 1. JOHN ELLIOTT

Birth Date:	1759
Birth Place:	COUNTY DONEGAL, IRELAND
Christen Date:	12
Christen Place:	Elliottstown?
Death Date:	16 Mar 1809
Death Place:	COUNTY DONEGAL, IRELAND
Burial Place:	KILLYBEGS, DONEGAL COUNTY, IRELAND
Occupation:	FARMER, SHIP CAPTAIN & METHODIST PREACHER (J. Lawrence,1968)
Education:	SCOTS-IRISH ANCESTRY
Religion:	METHODIST

Notes: JOHN ELLIOTT rests in the Methodist Cemetery, parish of Killybegs, county of Donegal (J. Lawrence, 1968). Death date: Mar 16, 1809, burial along with two infant children in Methodist Cemetery,Killybegs Lower, Main St., County of Donegal, Ireland. Ordnance Survey Sheet p. 73,74,82 in which town-land can be located. The Methodist Graveyard is separated from the Church. (Source: Donegal Genealogical Service. The Diamond, Lifford, Co., Donegal, Ireland). (Other Sources: 1. St. Catherines (old) Killybegs: IGRS Collection, GO 2. 1796 Spinning Wheel Premium Lists. Microfiche index in National Archives, comprising in the case of Donegal, over 14, 000 names. Farmers who planted required acreage in flax received a free spinning wheel from the Irish government. The government was stimulating the linen industry through an incentive program. 3. Conaghan, Pat., Bygones: New Horizons on the History of Killybegs, Killybegs, 1989.)

Spouse:	FRANCES "Fanny" BLAINE
Birth Date:	1 May 1764
Birth Place:	COUNTY DONEGAL, IRELAND
Christen Place:	DAUGHTER OF METHODIST PREACHER
Death Date:	28 Mar 1845
Death Place:	DOUGHTY CREEK, GEORGE'S HOME
Burial Date:	30 Mar 1845
Burial Place:	KENNE METHODIST CEMETERY
Occupation:	PIONEER AND MOTHER OF 15
Education:	SCOTS-IRISH ANCESTRY
Religion:	METHODIST
Spouse Father:	MOSES BLAINE (1730–)
Spouse Mother:	JANE MCKEE (1730–)

Spouse Notes: FRANCES BLAINE ELLIOTT.[42] After John, Fannie's husband died, Fanny gathered her courage and ventured into the new world by ship with 8 or 9 of her 13 living children, from Donegal, Ireland, to Baltimore, Maryland. From the harbor, they traveled the National Road, before it was a well-established roadway, westward to the Ohio River, then to Zanesville and north toward Indian country near today's Coshocton-Holmes County line. Here, she settled with her brood on land purchased for $1.25 an acre from the Scioto Co. The land, settled under the Land Ordinance of 1785, used the rectangular survey system. Land was divided into township tracts six miles square, and sub-divided into thirty-six 640-acre sections. This practice produced a nice profit for the land developer who paid 25 cents an acre, with a minimum down payment based on credit from the government. "Fannie was a widow who at the age of fifty-two came from Ireland to America bringing nine of her younger children with her. In July of 1816 (the year without summer) they left the town of Ardara in the parish of Killibegs in the county of Donegal in the north of Ireland and sailed from Londonderry." In fact, the ship headed for New York City, but bad weather forced them off course. They landed in Baltimore after nearly twelve weeks of tormented travel in which sleeping on deck was preferred to avoid being tossed out of bed by rough seas. (Lawrence, 1968) They came directly from Baltimore by four-horse wagon. They walked over the Allegheny mountains to a spot above present day Clark near where the Elliott Church stood. A story handed down through the family says that the Ohio River was the only water that their wagons had to be ferried across. (Lawrence, 1968) Fannie held 200 acres and son George held 100 acres in the same township. This land was then located in Coshocton county and would be until 1824, when a new county was formed in the north, Holmes County. While living here, the daughter Jane married Daniel Boyd in 1825, who was living with his father, Robert east of Keene. This was property the older folks (1960's) would know as the Everett Boyd farm. Daniel came to America a year or more before his family. He wanted to find his childhood sweetheart here in this "Garden of Eden". One European historian said 'This place called Ohio must be the spot of that Biblical Garden.' (Lawrence, 1968) The three Methodist families that contributed to the Keene Methodist Church were Elliott, Boyd and Finlay. These three families headed by John Elliott, Albert Boyd and George Finlay lived among each other over in Donegal County, Ireland. The wives of these three men were sisters and daughters of the ship captain Moses Blaine who was also a Methodist preacher. Quite naturally these folk on coming to America brought with them strong Methodist tendencies. They intermarried in Ireland and kept right at it here in America. (Lawrence, 1968) The third family, the Finlays, came from Ireland and settled in the same general territory above what was first called Bloomfield, and where the Elliotts had preceded them by a few years. Then, the Elliotts moved from Holmes County and settled on what in later years was known as the Matt Wheatcraft farm; the son George held the title and Frances Blaine, his mother, made this her home for the rest of her life. This farm paralleled the Chestnut Ridge Road on the east side. About all that remained to identify the farm was the old church building known as Elliott's Chapel, built on the corner of George Elliott's farm in 1862. The Chapel was destroyed for safety reasons in the 1950's. There was an Elliott Church (located in Mechanic Township., Holmes County, about 3 miles from Clark on Township road #85) as well as an Elliott Chapel (Mill Creek Township, Coshocton County. Township road #38 on the ridge just west of Ohio #83), both are gone. During the intervening years, strip mining changed the landscape dramatically. (Lawrence, 1968) Mill Creek (Range 6 Town 7) Township—located in the southwest corner of the Township, the Frances Blaine Elliott family purchased the land (pieces 28 & 17) in George Elliott's name. George purchased the Township corner (piece 30) in addition. (Atlas of Coshocton County, Ohio, from a survey by B.J. Lake, C.E., 1872. Published by C.O. Titus 320 Chestnut St. Philadelphia, PA)[40]

Marriage Date:	25 Aug 1781
Marriage Place:	ARDARA, DONEGAL, IRELAND
Children:	JAMES
	MOSES
	JOHN (Twin)
	MARY (Twin)
	SIMON
	ANDREW
	CHARLES
	JOHN (DEACON)
	GEORGE
	SAMUEL
	ANNE
	JANE
	NANCY
	THOMAS
	SIMON

(2) 1.1 JAMES ELLIOTT

Birth Date:	21 Aug 1782
Birth Place:	ARDARA, DONEGAL, IRELAND
Christen Place:	IN 1817 FOLLOWED REST OF FAMILY TO OHIO
Death Date:	7 Sep 1849
Death Place:	WOODHILL FARM, MECHANICS TWP, HOLMES CO
Burial Place:	ELLIOTT CHURCH, HOLMES CO. (see Map)

Occupation:	OWNER/FARMER at Woodhill FARM, KEENE, OHIO
Education:	IRELAND
Religion:	METHODIST

Notes: JAMES ELLIOTT: the oldest of the sons, James, Moses and Andrew and daughter, Mary, stayed behind in Ireland. The three sons came in 1819 and the daughter Mary died in Ireland. (Lawrence, 1968)

James Elliott was elected Coroner, Mechanic Township 1832–1834, Justice of the Peace Mechanic Township 1829–32. His will was probated September 14, 1849 in Holmes County, Ohio. The letter which follows was written by James Elliot(t) to his brother-in-law Daniel Boyd and his wife (James sister) Jane from his farm, Woodhill, dated 11th April 1842.

My dear Brother and Sister,

For the first time I believe in my life I write to you to inform you how we all are getting along. All our Families now are in tolerable good health except my Brother Thomas' Family. Lucy has been confined to her bed these many months but she has recovered so far that she bore to be removed to my Brother Sams's on last Friday and it was a great undertaking. She has had another boy (Thomas) about two weeks ago and considering her weak helpless condition the child seems to do well. Her mother has taken the baby (Thomas) and the other two youngest children (Newton and Nathan) home and the two oldest is with us (Simon and Daniel). Tom has sold his barn and lot for 800 dollars and his Father in Law has also sold and they all mean to start for the Ioway territory as soon as their health will permit which will be some time as Tom and all the Family was all so bad about a month ago that one could not give the other a drink but they are recovering fast. A great many has died with a complaint they call lung fever and the scarlet fever has also carried away a great many children and grown people. My son Tom got married on the 10th Feb to Mary, Williams Mott's Daughter, and lives in the house with us yet. They will take up for themselves after harvist. George David Elliot(t) and Richard _____James has rented his farm for two years and gets the _____half, We have 70 acres of wheat in this year and James 20 all of which looks well some of it, too well. So if we run? we will have a heavy harvist. Jamese's child is doing well but very troublesome. _____looks bad this child wore her down more than all the children she ever had. Your Brother Robert has rented your Brother Johns farm and has moved to it a few days ago. Wm. Dunkans Children had all the measles lately but they are recovering. My Mother is as well as she has been any time these 7 years. I intend going if alive and well to go to see you all in the fall and stay until you are tired of me. Eliza gets along finely and I believe quite contented. Edwards wife has got a fine boy he was nearly trampling us all under his feet when it was born. Uncle always asks him how his yellow boy comes on. I think he does not take it very well. Wheat is now 90 cents at Lewisville (Roscoe Village) we expect it will be a dollar when the boats will begin to run which will be next week. There never was such appearance of wheat in this neighborhood and a great dale (deal) of it sown. The family had a letter from their Brother he is near Bedford. He gives an account of Betty and Tom Anderson. Tom has signed the pledge as they call it and is doing better. It mentions Bill Walker which says he is doing well and out of debt but dont say anything about any one else except it would had saved me a great dale(deal) of trouble and my Brother _____ will have to do the same. I understand my Brother Andy is about settling out for 1000 dollars. We had a revival in our class at new years. 25 have joined among whom were old Bitney(?) and his son David and Eliza Jane _____ Caskey and his two sons and Daughter Wm. Dunk(an?) has also joined and George Elliot(t)'s Daughter Jane. Such a whillabalew(!) as we had you scarsely ever seen or heard. The temperance course is making great progress both in Holmes and Coshocton Counties. I have a barrel of good hard cider lying in the posnage? (parsonage) and no one goes near it. That mother whose child is "wearing her down" says its a fine thing she will soon have plenty of good vinegar. When George went to the seminary last May he got under conviction the first night and got through in two or three days. You won't think he was not the same person when he comes home. James thinks he must preach what is the reason he goes to the seminary, and the children made better? progress in learning. Beg to be remembered to every one of you and am my dear brother your very affectionate.

(signed) James Elliot(t)

The land on which the Elliotts settled in Coshocton County, Ohio, lay mostly on the divide between Tom's Run and Military Creek. These lots were almost contiguous and extended in a northerly direction from Lot 25 in the south:

1. From Lot 25 settled by James Elliott in 1819 to the lots of Andrew Elliott's 140–acre farm was a distance of almost two miles.

2. George Elliott Sr. (Blacksmith George) settled on Lot 24 in 1819. After living there for 35 years, he transferred ownership to his eldest son Robert who

lived there 1900. At the time of the transfer, George bought the west half of Lot 18 and lived there until his death in 1868.

3. Samuel Elliott, a son of George and brother of Robert settled on Lot 19 that Andrew Elliott first bought. He settled there and later bought Lot 20.

4. Andrew's oldest son when married purchased the Lot laying directly west of Andrew's.

5. Andrew's second son, James C. bought Lot "1 laying just west of Lot 19 and lived thereon until his death in 1880. He seemed to have been a very progressive farmer having two fair sized orchards with various kinds of delicious fruit. He also had a large two-story frame house, a frame outhouse into which he had running water piped from a spring some distance northeast of the house. About 3 years after his death, A.W. Logsdon and purchased the farm.

(Source: description by A.W. Logsdon's son, Harry C. Logsdon, author of Silent Streams.)

Spouse:	MARY HESTER STEVENSON
Birth Date:	1780
Birth Place:	DONEGAL, IRELAND
Christen Place:	WITH FOUR CHILDREN
Death Date:	13 May 1868
Death Place:	WOODHILL FARM
Burial Place:	ELLIOTT CHURCH, HOLMES CO., NEXT TO HUSBAND
Occupation:	IRISH HEIRESS?
Education:	SISTER OF ANDREW'S WIFE, ANNA S. STEVENSON
Religion:	METHODIST
Spouse Father:	James STEVENSON Rev.
Spouse Mother:	Elizabeth Nesbitt

Spouse Notes: In a letter from Mary Ann Boyd to her parents at home in Coolville, (23 Mar 1849), she reported visiting aunts and uncles in Keene. Uncle James gave her a good kiss and next a pinch of snuff. He has been quite unwell but is now much better. Aunt Hester is in a bad condition indeed. She can get from the bed to the fire, and don't leave her bedroom at all, she says she feels a great deal of pain.

Marriage Date:	1800
Marriage Place:	DONEGAL, IRELAND
Children:	JOHN NESBIT
	ANN JANE
	JAMES JR.
	Elizabeth "ELIZA"
	HESTER
	FRANCES "Fannie"
	THOMAS "Tom"
	GEORGE NESBIT
	MOSES

(3) 1.1.1 JOHN NESBIT ELLIOTT

Birth Date:	4 Aug 1807
Birth Place:	Adara, COUNTY DONEGAL, IRELAND
Death Date:	8 Dec 1877
Death Place:	ROCKFORD TWP, CALDWELL CO.,MO
Burial Place:	Kingston Cemetery, Caldwell Co., MO

Notes: The family moved to Mirabile, Missouri in 1868. (Getrude Croft, 1969) In the Spring of 1834, James and John took two teams of horses and wagons to Jefferson County to bring the John Finlay families to Holmes County. The family lived for a year in the house of my father's cousin, James Elliott. Father was his godfather at his baptism. During July of that summer, Alice married John Graham, July 7, 1834.
(Source: Record of the Finlay Family as given by Mary Finlay Hester, Jan. 30, 1903)

Spouse:	ISABELLE DUNCAN
Birth Date:	11 Jun 1811
Death Date:	4 Mar 1885
Death Place:	ROCKFORD TWP, CALDWELL CO., MO
Spouse Father:	Andrew DUNCAN
Spouse Mother:	Jane Wiley

Spouse Notes: In October, 1870, Mr. Boyd was married to Miss Elmira, daughter of John N. and Isabel (Duncan) Elliott. They came originally from Holmes County, Ohio, settled in Rockford Township, in this county in 1868. Mr. and Mrs. Boyd have two children: William Rollin and Elmira. Mr.B's homestead is situated about three-fourths of a mile from Mirabile, and is a well-improved farm of 170 acres.
Source: Karen Walker.

Marriage Date:	22 Nov 1830
Marriage Place:	OHIO? or Nov 27, 1830 Holmes Co. Records

Children:	THOMAS
	ANDREW
	JAMES
	WILLIAM W.
	NANCY
	ELMIRA
	GEORGE NESBIT

(3) 1.1.2 ANN JANE ELLIOTT

Birth Date:	1811
Birth Place:	1812?—Donegal, Ireland
Death Date:	4 Mar 1838
Death Place:	27 years old

Burial Place:	Elliott Church Cemetery, Mechanic Twp, Holmes Co., OH
Occupation:	Buried next to James and Hester in the Elliott Church yard

(3) 1.1.3 JAMES JR. ELLIOTT Rev.

Birth Date:	13 Jun 1813
Birth Place:	Donegal, Ireland
Death Date:	2 May 1870
Burial Place:	probably at Doylestown, Wayne Co., OH

Notes: *James has rented his farm for two years and get the ___half, we have 70 acres and James 20 all of which looks well some of it, too well. So if we run? we will have a heavy harvist. Jamese's child is doing well but very troublesome. ___looks bad this child wore her down more than all the other children she ever had.* (James Elliott letter to the Boyds, 11 Apr., 1842) He married Hester Duncan, b. 1816, d. Sep 9, 1841, m. Dec 17, 1835 burial—Elliott's Church, Holmes County, Ohio (Source: Getrude Croft based on Holmes Co., records). He later married Mary Franks in 1851(?).

In the Spring of 1834, James and John took two teams of horses and wagons to Jefferson Co. to bring the John Finlay families to Holmes Co. The family lived for a year in the house of my father's cousin, James Elliott. Father was his godfather at his baptism. During July of that summer Alice married John Graham, July 7, 1834. (Source: Record of the Finlay Family as given by Mary Finlay Hester, Jan. 30, 1903)

Spouse:	Sarah Barnhill

Marriage Date:	7 Jun 1849
Marriage Place:	Holmes Co., OH. R. Shepler, Minister

(3) 1.1.4 Elizabeth "ELIZA" ELLIOTT

Birth Date:	1816
Birth Place:	Donegal, Ireland

| Death Date: | 28 Nov 1884 |
| Burial Place: | probably in Westfield, Illinois |

| Spouse: | Alexander Collins Rev. |
| Religion: | United Brothern Minister |

| Marriage Date: | 21 Mar 1841 |
| Marriage Place: | Holmes County, OH by M. Chapman, J.P. |

(3) 1.1.5 HESTER ELLIOTT

| Birth Date: | 1817 |
| Birth Place: | Donegal, Ireland |

(3) 1.1.6 FRANCES "Fannie" ELLIOTT

Birth Date:	20 Feb 1818
Birth Place:	Donegal, IRELAND
Death Date:	19 Feb 1888
Burial Place:	Elliott Church, Holmes Co., OH

Spouse:	WILLIAM DUNCAN
Birth Date:	8 Jul 1806
Birth Place:	HARRISON CO., OH? OR PA
Death Date:	30 Dec 1875
Death Place:	1876?
Burial Place:	Elliott Church, Holmes Co., OH

| Marriage Date: | 4 Feb 1836 |
| Marriage Place: | HOLMES CO., OH, JOHN ARMOR, J.P. |

Children: THOMAS E.

                        HESTER JANE

                        MARY A.

                        ANDREW

                        ELIZA S.

                        FRANCES A.

                        JAMES E.

                        ELMIRA E.

                        WILLIAM E. (BILLY)

                        JOHN STEVENSON

                        EMMA B.

                        GEORGE A.

(3) 1.1.7 THOMAS "Tom" ELLIOTT

Birth Date:	1 May 1821
Birth Place:	PROBABLY IN WHAT IS NOW HOLMES CO.,OH
Death Date:	3 Feb 1903
Death Place:	DEFIANCE CO., OH
Burial Place:	Independence, OH

Notes: James wrote: *"My son Tom got married on the 10th Feb (1843) to Mary, William Mott's Daughter, and lives in the house (Woodhill) with us yet. They will take up for themselves after harvist. They moved to Defiance Oh in 1843* (Source: G. Croft, 1963).

Spouse:	MARY MOTT
Birth Date:	1825
Birth Place:	ABT 1825
Death Date:	16 May 1896

Death Place: Defiance, OH

Burial Place: Independence, OH

Spouse Notes: Mary William according to G. Croft 1963.

Marriage Date: 10 Feb 1843

Marriage Place: Woodhill, Keene, Ohio

(3) 1.1.8a GEORGE NESBIT ELLIOTT Judge*

Birth Date: 10 Jul 1824

Birth Place: Holmes County, Ohio

Death Date: 28 Dec 1899

Death Place: Topeka, Shawnee Co., KS

Occupation: JUDGE, prob bar Topeka, Kans.

Notes: George went from Ohio to California soon after the discovery of gold. He made a fortune which he invested in a small vessel and stocked with a cargo of merchandise. The crew mutinied and casting him on a rocky island in the Pacific Ocean, sailed away. He was rescued b a passing vessel and returned to Ohio engaged in the practice of the law. He married and located to Warrensburg, Missouri. Later, he moved with his family to Topeka, Kansas and served for some years as probated judge of Shawnee County. He died in Topeka about 1890, leaving a family.
(source: "Several Ancestral Lines of James P. Refrew and His Wife, Ella Black" by James P. Renfrew, Alva OK, Alva Record Print, Alva OK, age 70.)[55] from Karen Lee (Hill) Walker.

Spouse: MARY EMMA DAVID

Birth Date: 30 Nov 1838

Death Date: 10 Mar 1909

Occupation: 3 CHILDREN, CHARLES, LULU, BESSIE ESTER

Other spouses: ELMIRA EVAN

(3) 1.1.8b GEORGE NESBIT ELLIOTT Judge*

(See above)

Spouse:	ELMIRA EVAN
Death Date:	11 Feb 1849
Marriage Date:	6 May 1849
Marriage Place:	Coshocton County Records
Other spouses:	MARY EMMA DAVID

(3) 1.1.9 MOSES ELLIOTT

Birth Date:	21 Mar 1826
Birth Place:	Holmes Co., OH
Death Date:	27 Jan 1895
Death Place:	Warensburg, MO
Burial Place:	Sunset Cem., Warrensburg, MO
Occupation:	Farmer

Notes: He lived on what became the Keifer farm in Holmes Co., (H.C. Logsdon, 1941) Moses moved his family west to Warrensburg, Missouri in 1872. They are both buried in Warrensburg as well as all their children and grandchildren. (source: J..Lell Elliott, Jr. in a letter to Dr. A.W. Elliott, Mar 6, 1966)

Spouse:	MARTHA A. FRIZELL
Birth Date:	1 May 1831
Death Date:	3 Aug 1910
Death Place:	Warensburg, MO
Burial Place:	Sunset Cem., Warrensburg, MO
Spouse Father:	John FRIZELL

Marriage Date: 12 Apr 1849

Marriage Place: Holmes County Records

Children: Elmyra

                      Mary

                      James B.

                      Emma

                      Martha (Twin)

                      JOHN FRIZELL (Twin)

                      Frances Cora Warner

(2) 1.2 MOSES ELLIOTT

Birth Date: 1 Feb 1784

Birth Place: DONEGAL, IRELAND

Christen Place: 1819—SETTLED IN ATHENS CO., OH

Death Date: 19 Dec 1854

Death Place: PIONEER FARM IN CARTHAGE TOWNSHIP

Burial Place: Meigs-Athens Co. line

Occupation: FARMER, JUSTICE OF THE PEACE

Education: IRELAND

Religion: METHODIST

Notes: MOSES ELLIOTT—born February 1, 1784, in the county of Donegal, Ireland, came to the United States in 1819, and settled as a farmer in Carthage Township in 1823. He lived on the farm where first settled, till his death in 1854. He was a Justice of the Peace for twelve years, and was highly respected as a citizen. His family, two sons and five daughters, were all living in 1869. (Walker, History of Athens County, 1869)

Three of the older sons of John and Fanny Blaine Elliott, James, Moses and Andrew, stayed behind in Ireland, also a daughter as well as two infants buried beside her husband. The three sons came in 1819 and the daughter Mary died in

Ireland. (Lawrence, 1968) Samuel wrote to Daniel Boyd (16 Jun 1842) saying that "Mother's (Fannie Blaine Elliott) health is as usual she wishes to know when you (Daniel) and Jane will be to see her and wishes to be remembered to Moses and wife and family." Moses and his family were living near Coolville, Ohio.

Spouse:	JANE CUSCADEN
Birth Date:	1785
Birth Place:	ABT 1785?
Christen Place:	THEY ARRIVED IN OHIO IN 1819
Education:	Mother of 2 boys and 5 girls (names?)

Spouse Notes: Checked with Historical Society in Athens, Ohio.—found no information on wife and daughters. (ESE–11/17/93)

Marriage Date:	1815
Marriage Place:	DONEGAL, IRELAND
Children:	JOHN
	JAMES

(3) 1.2.1 JOHN ELLIOTT

Birth Date:	1 May 1816
Birth Place:	Killybegs, DONEGAL, IRELAND May 25 or May 1?
Death Date:	29 May 1879
Death Place:	Jasper Co., MO
Burial Place:	Webb City Cemetery, MO
Occupation:	FARMER, COUNTY COMMISSIONER
Education:	CARTHAGE TWSP, OHIO IN 1823, TIL 1859
Religion:	Spring River, JASPER CO., MO, 7 miles west of Carthage

Notes: John Elliott, the oldest son of Moses Elliott, was born in Ireland in 1816. He came to Carthage, Ohio with his father's family in 1823, and lived there until 1859. He was County Commissioner several years and much esteemed. In 1859, he removed to Southwestern Missouri, where he still resided in 1869. During the Civil War he was driven from his farm on account of his Union sentiments, and was absent several years, but returned after the end of hostilities. (Walker, History of Athens County, 1869, pp. 457)

Christen: SETTLED IN CARTHAGE IN 1823, TIL 1859
Death: SOUTHWEST, MISSOURI

(L.L. Thompson.) Her grandmother, Lora Elliott Storm(s) was raised by Moses and Laura Elliott. She was the daughter of Robert Lee Storm(s) and Addie Miller. She also had a twin brother, Robert Lee Storm(s); a sister, Jeanette; a brother, Leslie; and I think there was another brother named Arthur. I really don't think my grandmother's middle name was Elliott, I think she just used it in her adult life. Addie Miller Storms died when my grandmother was eight years old and her father took her and her siblings to Washington state. My grandmother and her twin brother did not stay there very long. They came back to Missouri and her twin brother was raised by Robert Lee Storm(s)' brother, George Porter Storms and his wife Laura Bell Storm(s). My grandmother was raised by Moses Elliott and Laura Stults Elliott. She always referred to them as Aunt Laura and Uncle Moses and none of us EVER questioned just what the actual relationship was. Just recently, I located a distant cousin I knew as a child who has promised to send me some information. Haven't heard from her yet, but during out telephone conversation, she read some passages from a family history account she has in her possession that refers to Moses Elliott as Addie Miller's "mother's uncle." I have some information on the Storm(s), but the Millers and the Elliotts are extremely elusive.

Moses Elliott's father was John Elliott (1816–1879), born 25 May, 1816, County Donegal, Ireland; died 29 May 1879, Jasper County, Missouri. He is buried in the Webb City Cemetery. His wife was Charlotte Mansfield, born 28 September, Queen Anne County, Maryland; died 31 December 1883, Jasper County, Missouri. She is also buried in the Webb City Cemetery. Moses Elliott (1848–1918) was born in 1848 and died in 1918 and is also buried in Webb City. His wife, Laura, was born in 1860. She, too,is buried in WebbCity. (Source:?)

Koskioco Elliott, the present surveyor of Jasper county, who is familiarly known as "Kos" Elliott, was born in Athens county, Ohio, Oct.23, 1843, removing from the old Ohio home at the age of fifteen with his father to Jasper County, near the post-office of Sherwood. Having returned to Ohio, he enlisted in 1864 in the One Hundred and Seventy-fourth Ohio, serving the residue of the war. He was married June 24, 1874, to L.L. Johns, a native of Mercer County, Ohio. Her birthday was February 28, 1843. They have but one child, whose name is Mary L. Elliott. Our subject is a member of the Grange and has been County Surveyor for more than ten years, an office of no little responsibility and public service. Mr. Elliott resides upon the farm formerly owned by the father of Mrs. Elliott, Mr. A. L. Johns, who was a pioneer in Iowa, as his daughter attended school in a log schoolhouse where the city of Des Moines, Iowa, now stands. Mrs. Elliott's father and mother, Mr. and Mrs. Johns, died on the home farm where she now lives and are buried in the cemetery nearby called "Hoosier Point Cemetery," named from the point of timber near by the cemetery. Mr. Elliott's father, John Elliott, was a native of Ireland, Kellybegs, County Donegal, "where they eat potatoes, skins and all," who came to America in 1819, at the age of three years. His uncle, Charles Elliott, D.D., was for many years editor of the Western Christian Advocate and the Central Christian Advocate at another time, and later was president of the Wesleyan University of Iowa. He was also author of "Elliott on Slavery" and "History of the Great Secession of Methodism" in 1856, predicting the secedence of the Southern states at no distant day. There is only one copy of the book in the county, which is in the Lincoln Township library, established by James Haley, he having given one hundred and sixty acres of land for the purpose. Mr. Elliott's farm of 150 acres is in sections 7 and 12, Township 29, range 32 and 33, and has on it a small orchard besides other improvements.

Moses Elliott—One of the well known old settlers of Jasper County, Missouri, whose home has been here since 1859, is Moses Elliott, who resides on section 36, in Mineral Township. His birth was in Athens County, Ohio, on February 4, 1849, and he was a son of John Elliott, who was born in Killybegs, County Donegal, Ireland, on May 1, 1816, and came to America, locating first in Washington County, Pennsylvania, later removing to Athens County, Ohio, in the early days of its settlement. John Elliott remained in Ohio until 1859, at this date coming to Jasper County, Missouri, and locating near Spring River, seven miles west of Carthage, and died on his farm there, in 1879.

The mother of our subject was formerly Charlotta Mansfield, who was a daughter of Thomas Mansfield, who had been a soldier in the Revolutionary war, and his widow received a pension on that account. The Mansfields came of an old and distinguished family of Maryland. Nine children were born to the parents of our subject, and of such sturdy constitution that all grew to maturity, our subject being the fourth in order of age. He was but ten years old when the family removal was made to Jasper County, and here he attended school, remaining with his parents until 1861. At that time he went back to Ohio and remained there until 1865, but then returned to Jasper County and engaged in farming until 1875, when he went to Arizona and began mining. For the following five years he continued to mine, and then came back to his farm, in Jasper County. In 1885 he found the first lead on his land and began mining, also continued in farming.

Mr. Elliott was married in 1890 to Miss Laura Stults, who is a native of Springfield, Illinois, where she was reared and educated, and she was a daughter of J.W. Stults, who was a native of Kentucky and was one of the early settlers of Jasper County. Since 1896 Mr. Elliott has been a Democrat, and is one of the best known among the early residents of the county.

Spouse:	CHARLOTTE MANSFIELD
Birth Date:	28 Sep 1816
Birth Place:	Queen Anne Co, MD
Death Date:	31 Dec 1883
Death Place:	Jasper Co., MO
Burial Place:	Webb City Cemetery, MO
Occupation:	HOME MAKER
Education:	Koskioco, Alice, Mary, Moses, Charles, Ann, Sarah and?
Spouse Father:	THOMAS MANSFIELD

Spouse Notes: Spouse Notes: Charlotta Mansfield was a daughter of Thomas Mansfield, who had been a soldier in the Revolutionary War, and his widow received a pension on that account. The Mansfields came of an old and distinguished family of Maryland. John married Charlotte in about 1836? She was born in Maryland. They had nine children: Koskioco "Kos", Alice, Mealy, Moses, Charles, Ann, Sarah and Jenny and one more. (Source: Linda L. Thompson 5/27/97)

Marriage Date:	1836
Marriage Place:	ATHENS CO., OH OR MARYLAND?
Children:	KOSKIOCO "Kos"
	Mary
	Alice
	MOSES
	Charles
	Ann
	Sarah
	JANE

(3) 1.2.2 JAMES ELLIOTT

Birth Date:	1826
Birth Place:	PIONEER FARM, CARTHAGE TOWNSHIP
Christen Place:	ATHENS COUNTY, OHIO
Death Date:	1890
Occupation:	TOWNSHIP CLERK

Notes: James Elliott—youngest son of Moses Elliott, was born in Carthage in 1826, and has lived ever since on the farm where he was born. He has been township clerk from many years and is held in high esteem in the community. (Walker, History of Athens County, 1869, pp. 457)

(2) 1.3 JOHN ELLIOTT

Birth Date:	5 Mar 1786
Death Date:	1786
Death Place:	DIED IN INFANCY
Occupation:	TWIN OF MARY LIVED ONLY SHORT TIME

(2) 1.4 MARY ELLIOTT

Birth Date:	5 Mar 1786
Birth Place:	DONEGAL, IRELAND
Christen Place:	LEFT A DAUGHTER, ISABELLA
Death Date:	1816
Death Place:	DONEGAL, IRELAND
Burial Place:	Killybegs Methodist Cemetery
Occupation:	DIED YOUNG IN IRELAND
Education:	STAYED BEHIND WITH TWO OLDER BROTHERS
Religion:	METHODIST

Notes: Three of the older sons, James, Moses and Andrew stayed behind in Ireland, also a daughter was well as two infants buried beside her husband. The three sons came in 1819 and the daughter Mary died in Ireland. (Lawrence, 1968)

Mary was a twin of John (3) who died in infancy. Mary married James McKee and had one daughter, Isabella, who married—Walker and came to America in 1845, as a widow. She was a Methodist and lived in Coshocton and Defiance Co. OH. (Melvin/Elaine Elliott, 1998)

Spouse:	JAMES MCKEE
Birth Date:	1785
Marriage Date:	6 Jun 1803
Marriage Place:	Donegal, Ireland
Children:	ISABELLA

(3) 1.4.1 ISABELLA McKEE

Birth Date:	1 Jun 1803
Birth Place:	Ardara, Killybegs, Donegal, Ireland
Christen Place:	A WIDOW WITH 2 CHILDREN

Death Date:	6 Apr 1885
Death Place:	DEFIANCE CO., OH
Religion:	Methodist

Notes: Isabella, who married—Walker and came to America in 1845, as a widow. She was a Methodist and lived in Coshocton and Defiance Co. Ohio.

Spouse:	WILLIAM? WALKER
Birth Date:	1802
Birth Place:	ABT 1802?
Death Date:	1828
Death Place:	ABT?

Spouse Notes: William? Walker drowned in Ireland while cutting lake ice for storage, according Goller family tradition. (E. Kintner and G. Snyder, p. 204)

Marriage Date:	1825/1827
Children:	WILLIAM "Billy"
	Mary

(2) 1.5 SIMON ELLIOTT

Birth Date:	25 Dec 1787
Birth Place:	IRELAND
Death Date:	22 Dec 1808
Death Place:	IRELAND

(2) 1.6 ANDREW ELLIOTT

Birth Date:	5 May 1790
Birth Place:	CAME TO AMERICA IN 1819
Christen Place:	Burial: KEENE METHODIST

Death Date:	13 May 1862
Death Place:	RETURNED TO COSHOCTEN, OHIO
Burial Place:	METHODIST CEMETERY, KEENE, OHIO
Occupation:	WHEELWRIGHT, farmer
Education:	BOUND FOR MISSOURI 1842
Religion:	Methodist

Notes: ANDREW—One of the older sons, James, Moses and Andrew, who stayed behind in Ireland. The three sons came to Ohio in 1819. The daughter Mary died in Ireland. (Lawrence, 1968) Andrew and James married sisters in Ireland and through their wives were heir to a fortune in Ireland, but being Elliotts and unconcerned about wealth they never bothered to get the fortune (p. 15 Blanche Elliott, 1941).

In a letter to his sister, Samuel wrote that "Andrew sold his place for one thousand dollars and is bound for Missouri". (Samuel Elliott, in a letter dated June 16th 1842) Andrew must have traveled to Iowa to settle for a time, where his wife Anna S. Stevenson died and was buried at Quaspueton, Iowa. He returned to Coshocton County. Andrew lies buried in the Keene Methodist Cemetery next to his daughter, Hester. The headstone carries both Andrew and Hester's date of death and age. The headstone was placed on the grave site at a later date by Hester's husband, Albert Mansford. Probably, both names were placed on the same stone as a measure of love and economy.

Spouse:	ANNA S. STEVENSON
Birth Date:	1796
Death Date:	1843
Death Place:	IOWA TERRITORY
Burial Place:	QUASPUETON, IOWA
Occupation:	SISTER OF HESTER, JAMES' WIFE
Education:	IRELAND
Religion:	METHODIST
Spouse Father:	James STEVENSON Rev.
Spouse Mother:	Elizabeth Nesbitt

Spouse Notes: ANNA S. STEVENSON married Andrew in 1835? when they took up farming as a way to make a living. They had a daughter, Hester, born in 1836. In 1842, they decided to head west for Missouri to seek their fortune. They traveled to Quaspueton, Iowa, where Anna died and was buried in a local cemetery. Hester and her father returned to Keene, where she met and married, Albert Mansford. (ESE 11/17/93)

Quaspueton is located on the Wapsipincon River, about 25 miles east of Water-loo, Iowa. (Exit route 282 south from Interstate 20)

Marriage Date:	1815
Marriage Place:	???
Children:	HESTER

(3) 1.6.1 HESTER ELLIOTT

Birth Date:	14 Jun 1836
Christen Place:	HEADSTONE: HESTER AND FATHER ANDREW
Death Date:	7 Jul 1863
Death Place:	AGE 27 YR 23 DA
Burial Place:	METHODIST CEMETERY, KEENE, OHIO
Occupation:	WIFE
Spouse:	ALBERT MANSFORD

Spouse Notes: Loved his wife, Hester. Placed a headstone that included the name of Hester and her father, Andrew, in the Methodist Cemetery, Keene, Ohio.

(2) 1.7 CHARLES ELLIOTT D.D. LLD

Birth Date:	12 May 1792
Birth Place:	May 16(or May 12), 1792 in Glenconway, Donegal
Christen Date:	1811
Christen Place:	ELLIOTSTOWN, ADRARA, GLENCONWELL, IRELAND

Death Date:	6 Jun 1869
Death Place:	MOUNT PLEASANT, Henry Co., IOWA
Burial Date:	9 Jun 1869
Burial Place:	FOREST HOME CEMETERY
Occupation:	MISSIONARY, PROFESSOR, PREACHER, EDITOR, COLLEGE PRESIDENT
Education:	D. D., LLD. Madison College, Uniontown, PA
Religion:	METHODIST (licensed to preach in 1813)

Notes: CHARLES ELLIOTT. Methodist preacher, editor and President of Iowa Wesleyan University. He lived in Cincinnati, Ohio, Mount Pleasant, Iowa, and other places. Charles, one of Frances Blaine's older sons, was one of the earlier circuit riders at Keene and elsewhere and became rather famous in Methodism throughout the Central West. He was a co-founder of Ohio Wesleyan as well as President of Iowa Wesleyan. He was editing a Methodist paper as well as teaching at the same time. Simon, a younger brother, was also a well known Methodist. Before Charles started out as an itinerant preacher, he and his younger brother George were school teachers in Keene, Clark, Mill Creek and Bethlehem township schools. (Lawrence, 1968)

"In 1858 the trustees of Iowa Wesleyan elected as president the Rev. Charles Elliott D.D., LL.L. who had joined the faculty earlier as Professor of Ecclesiastical History and Biblical Literature. Previous presidents had been young men, beginning their careers, whereas Dr. Elliott was sixty-six years old and had achieved national Methodist distinction as a religious journalist and church historian."

Charles Elliott was born May 16(or May 12), 1792 in Glenconway, Donegal County, Ireland, was converted to the Irish Wesleyan Society in 1811 and was licensed to preach in 1813. Since his religious affiliation prevented matriculation in the University of Dublin, he pursued a collegiate program of study independently. He came to the United States in 1814 and settled in Ohio where he was admitted to the Ohio Annual Conference of the M.E. Church in 1818 and assigned to the Zanesville Circuit. In 1822 he spent a year as a missionary to the Wyandotte Indian Nation at Upper Sandusky, which he described in his book Indian Missionary Reminiscences (1850), and in 1823 became Presiding Elder of the Ohio District. Turning to educational work, he served as Professor of Languages at Madison College, Uniontown, Pennsylvania from 1827–1831.

In 1828 and 1829, under Charles Elliot(t), there was a great revival, which lasted through the summer and winter, and there were about one hundred and fifty accessions to the church. This revival, under the same preacher, swept all Uniontown and Madison College, and hundreds were converted. This was said to have been the most remarkable revival of religion ever known in Uniontown, PA. (Ellis, Frank, History of Fayette Co., Vol 1–3, 688–689, 1882.) This institution of the Pittsburgh Annual Conference later merged with Allegheny College and existed until 1872. From 1831–1833, Dr. Elliott was Presiding Elder of the Pittsburgh District. Here he began a long career in religious journalism as editor of the Pittsburgh Conference Journal 1833–1834 and the Western Christian Advocate 1836–1848. He was noted for his vigorous handling of controversial topics of church and national life.

He held churches in Springfield and Xenia, Ohio from 1848–1852 but returned to the editorial chair of the Western Christian Advocate 1852–1856. During these years he published the first of his many books, The life of the Rev. Robert R. Roberts 1844, Delineation of Roman Catholicism 1841 and A History of the Great Secession From the Methodist Episcopal Church in the year 1855..."the Methodist Episcopal Church, South" 1855. The book on Romanism was for many decades a widely used polemic in American Protestant circles. The history of the formation of the Methodist Episcopal Church, South, although marked by Elliott's anti-slavery bias, is still a useful work of reference. His anti-slavery feelings were strongly expressed in the booklets, Slavery Contrary to the Spirit of Christianity and Sinfulness of American Slavery 1850.

In 1857, Dr. Elliott was invited by President Lucien W. Berry to join the faculty of Iowa Wesleyan University and founded the Biblical Department. From this position he became president in 1858, a position which he held until 1861 when he moved to St. Louis, Missouri as editor of the Central Christian Advocate, although he retained his professorship. Here he had a somewhat stormy career since Missouri was the dividing line of the two division of the Methodist Episcopal Church and of the slavery and anti-slavery regions. These years have been recounted by Frank C. Tucker in The Methodist Church in Missouri 1789–1939, published in 1966.

In 1863 Elliott returned to the Iowa Wesleyan presidency which he held until 1866 when ill health and age forced him to retire. He lived in Mount Pleasant until his death on January 6, 1869 and was buried in Forest HomeCemetery. His contacts were extremely wide and his name was known. Many details of his administration reveal his endeavor to bring the college into wider repute and sounder academic practice. He arranged for special ceremonies in 1859 when Lucy Webster Killpatrick was the first woman graduate; he designed an elaborate commencement program with a Latin title page in 1860; he opened a department of foreign languages with regular courses in French and German. This was made possible when he appointed to the faculty the Rev. Adam Miller, M.D., who had done pioneer work among German Methodists. Adam Miller's important book, Experiences of German Methodist Preachers, was published in 1859 with a Mount Pleasant date line and to this Dr. Elliott contributed an introduction. Elliott likewise attracted to Mount Pleasant the retired Methodist bishop, Leonidas L. Hamline for whom the Hamline Literary Society was named.

Dr. Elliott also presented for honorary degrees a number of important figures from the national scene: Benjamin F. Crary, President of Hamline University; Horatio N. Robinson, Professor of Mathematics at the United States Navel Academy; Robinson Scott, later a leading theologian of the Irish Wesleyan Church; Oliver M. Spencer, President of the State University of Iowa. Had Elliott been president at any other time than the Civil War period, his educational abilities would have created more rapid results. But he did exert upon the local scene an influence which was significant at the time. In his last years he published Southwestern Methodism, A History of the M.E. Church in the South–West 1844 to 1864, 1868.

Dr. Elliott's connections continued with the university through his children. One daughter, Phebe Leech Elliott was graduated in 1860; was Professor of English Literature and Preceptors 1864–1865 and served on the Board of Trustees from 1870–1875 while a resident of Mount Pleasant. A second daughter, Fannie, married the Rev. LeRoy Monroe Vernon of the class of 1860 who became superintendent of Methodist work in Italy 1871–1888. Vernon's daughter married an Italian poet, Angelo DeBossis, whose son Carlo DeBossis as a member of the Columbia University faculty visited Iowa Wesleyan in 1925.

Simon Charles Elliott, his son, married Francis Roads of the Class of 1869, who was one of the Seven Founders of the P.E.O. Sisterhood at Iowa Wesleyan. Francis Roads Elliott had an interesting career in art teaching and community service and biographical accounts appear in The History of the P.E.O. Sisterhood 1903 and in Winona Evans Reeves, The Story of P.E.O., 1869–1923. A memorial marker for her was placed in the Elliott family plot in the Forest Home Cemetery, Mount Pleasant, by the Supreme Chapter of the P.E.O Sisterhood in 1951." (L.S. Haselmayer, The Presidents' Iowa Wesleyan College, 1967)

Simon married _____ and had a daughter, Dorothy. She became one of the seven sisters of P.E.O., which originated at Mt. Pleasant, Iowa. She married twice, became Dorothy Canfield Fisher (Writer of Mystery). The Canfield family owned the Canfield Paper Company in upstate New York.

Charles Elliott lived in Uniontown prior to the time his mother and siblings came to the new world. He received ordination in the Methodist Church while he was still in Ireland (1813). Charles came to America in 1814 and was appointed Professor of Languages at Madison Academy in 1827. The earliest church organization in the Uniontown community was the Methodist Episcopal (1825). During those few years, he taught courses, recruited students, and ministered to the students in the school and people in the community. In 1828–29, under Charles Elliott, there was a great revival, which lasted through the summer and winter, and there were about one hundred and fifty accessions to the church. The revival swept all Uniontown and Madison College, and hundreds were converted. When Rev. H.B. Bascum resigned as president of Madison College in Spring 1829, Professor J. H. Fielding and Rev. Charles Elliott were placed in charge. Charles Elliott was described as a pure and simple scholar who loved learning for its own sake. He and his family lived in a red frame house near the college taking in several boarders including his younger brother, Simon. In 1832, Madison College changed from support by the Methodist Conference and continued under the Cumberland Presbyterian Church until 1872 when it closed for lack of funds. As the change occurred, Charles moved on to Cincinnati and further success. Charles Elliott's brogue was pure Irish…he was said to have red hair. (Source: Frank R. Elliott, MD in Chicago, IL, great-grandson in a letter to Mrs. Jonasson, dated 8/9/67. Frank did not provide his lineage)

References for this information:

Hadden, James. History of Uniontown, Pennsylvania, 1913. Reproduced by Unigrahic, Inc., 1978, pp. 490–492.

Ellis, Frank (ed). History of Fayette County, PA., with Biographical Sketches of many of its Pioneers and Prominent Men. (Vol 1–3), 1882, 315–316
The Uniontown Public Library (1996) was a new building located near downtown, about a block from Route 40, and the center of town.

Spouse:	PHEBE LEECH
Birth Date:	1802
Birth Place:	1803? IN SALEM, PA
Death Date:	1882
Death Place:	MT. PLEASANT, IOWA?
Burial Place:	FOREST HOME CEMETERY?
Occupation:	HOME MAKER
Religion:	METHODIST

Spouse Notes: PHEBE LEECH—mother of 9? children and wife of an active minister and church leader. They married as Charles began his work as a missionary with the Wyandotte Indians at Upper Sandusky, Ohio. (Source: Frank R. Elliott, M.D. grandson of Charles & Phebe, 8/9/67 in a letter to Mr. Johasson)

Marriage Date:	14 May 1822
Marriage Place:	SALEM, MERCER CO, PA
Children:	PHEBE LEECH
	FANNIE Blaine
	SIMON CHARLES
	MARY JANE
	SARAH Fielding
	John Fletcher
	Robert Hopkins
	Joshua Soule
	Charles

(3) 1.7.1 PHEBE LEECH ELLIOTT

Birth Date:	13 Jan 1839
Birth Place:	never married
Occupation:	PROFESSOR OF ENGLISH LITERATURE
Education:	1860 GRADUATE Iowa Wesleyan

Notes: Phebe Leech Elliott graduated from Iowa Wesleyan in 1860. She was Professor of English Literature and Preceptors 1864–1865 and served on the Board of Trustees from 1870–1875 while a resident of Mount Pleasant.

(3) 1.7.2 FANNIE Blaine ELLIOTT

Birth Date:	1836
Birth Place:	PITTSBURG, PA
Death Date:	1869
Death Place:	SEDALIA,MO

Notes: Fannie married the Rev. LeRoy Monroe Vernon of the class of 1860 who became superintendent of Methodist work in Italy 1871–1888. Their daughter married an Italian poet, Angelo DeBossis, who had a son Carlo DeBossis. He was a member of the Columbia University faculty who visited Iowa Wesleyan in 1925.

Spouse:	Rev. Leroy M. VERNON
Birth Date:	23 Apr 1838
Birth Place:	MOINTGOMERY CO. INDIANA
Death Date:	10 Aug 1896
Death Place:	SYRACUSE, N.Y.
Occupation:	Methodist Preacher & Missionary (Italy)
Education:	Iowa Wesleyan, 1860

Spouse Notes: Rev. LeRoy Monroe Vernon of the class of 1860 at Iowa Wesleyan. He became superintendent of Methodist work in Italy 1871–1888. Their daughter (name?????) married an Italian poet, Angelo DeBossis, whose son Carlo DeBossis as a member of the Columbus University faculty visited Iowa Wesleyan in 1925.

Marriage Date:	27 Nov 1860
Marriage Place:	MT. PLEASANT, IO

Children:	LILLIAN VERNON
	CHARLES ELLIOTT

(3) 1.7.3 SIMON CHARLES ELLIOTT

Death Place:	NEW YORK CITY
Burial Place:	THROGS' NECK, LONG ISLAND, N.Y.

Notes: Simon Charles Elliott married Francis Roads of the Class of 1869. She was one of the Seven Founders of the P.E.O. Sisterhood at Iowa Wesleyan College. Simon and Francis had a daughter, Dorothy. She became one of the seven sisters of PEO, which originated at Mt. Pleasant, Iowa. The daughter married twice, became Dorthy Canfield Fisher (Writer of Mystery). The Canfield family owned the Canfield Paper Co. in upstate New York.(source: Janet Ewing) Grandson of Simon Elliott: Frank R. Elliott, M.D., 707 North Fairbanks Court, Chicago, Ill, 60611 (as of 8/9/67)

Spouse:	FRANCIS ROADS
Burial Place:	Mount Pleasant, Iowa
Education:	CLASS OF 1869, IOWA WESLEYAN

Spouse Notes: Francis Roads was among the first women to graduate from Iowa Wesleyan College, Class of 1869. She was one of the Seven Founders of the P.E.O. Sisterhood at Iowa Wesleyan. Francis Roads Elliott had an interesting career in art teaching and community service. Biographical accounts appear in The History of the P.E.O. Sisterhood 1903 and in Winona Evans Reeves, The Story of P.E.O. 1869–1923.

A memorial marker for her was placed on the Elliott family plot in the Forest Home Cemetery, Mount Pleasant, by the Supreme Chapter of the P.E.O Sisterhood in 1951." (L.S. Haslemayer, The Presidents of Iowa Wesleyan College, 1967) Burial: Forest Home Cemetery?

Marriage Date:	1869
Marriage Place:	Mount Pleasant, Iowa
Children:	DOROTHY CANFIELD

(3) 1.7.4 MARY JANE ELLIOTT

Birth Date:	17 Mar 1826
Spouse:	JOHATHAN FORD CONREY
Birth Date:	1825
Occupation:	Methodist Episcopal Minister
Spouse Father:	James D. CONREY
Spouse Mother:	Anna Layman (–1848)

Spouse Notes: In 1841 John Ford Conrey was ordained and appointed to New Street, a black congregation in Cincinnati. Later he severed numerous congregations including: Franklin, Oxford, Hillsboro, Ripley, Wilmington, Christie Chapel (Cincinnati), Dayton, Springfield, Xenia, Piqua, Hartwell, Waynesville, and finally Urbana which became his final resting place in 1892. In 1846 he married Mary Jane Elliott, daughter of the abolitionist Rev. Charles Elliott DD, LL.D., Methodist leader, Wyandotte Indian Missionary, preacher, editor, writer, author of Sinfulness of American Slavery published in Cincinnati in 1850 for the Methodist church and President of the Iowa Wesleyan University. Rev. Elliott's family settled in Coshocton County, Ohio. Siebert's list confirms Elliott family involvement in the UGRR(Underground Railroad) in Coshocton.
Source: 1/10/01—Jill Dunlap, Narrative for the Spread Eagle
Copyright ¬© 1999 edeena By Jill Vaught Dunlap Butler, Clermont, Brown County Coordinator, FOFS/Ohio Underground Railroad Association

Marriage Date: 26 Mar 1846

Children: JAMES ELLIOTT

                    CHARLES FORD

                    DAVID WILLIE

(3) 1.7.5 SARAH Fielding ELLIOTT

Birth Date: 1827

Spouse: J.F. DAWSON REV.

Birth Date: 1825

Birth Place: ABT

(3) 1.7.6 John Fletcher ELLIOTT

Education: mentioned in will

Spouse: Jane Yates

(3) 1.7.7 Robert Hopkins ELLIOTT

Spouse: Lydia Patterson

(3) 1.7.8 Joshua Soule ELLIOTT

(3) 1.7.9 Charles ELLIOTT, Jr.

(2) 1.8a JOHN (DEACON) ELLIOTT*

Birth Date: 29 Mar 1795

Birth Place: DONELGAL, IRELAND

Christen Place: LIVED IN THE TOWN OF COSHOCTON, OHIO

Death Date:	2 Sep 1868
Death Place:	COSHOCTON CO., OH
Burial Place:	OAK RIDGE C., COSHOCTON, OHIO
Occupation:	CARPENTER-PRESBYTERIAN & SHOE MAKER
Education:	CAME TO AMERICA prior to 1816
Religion:	PRESBYTERIAN "REBEL" MILL CREEK

Notes: JOHN ELLIOTT. John was the brother called 'Rebel' John since he was the only Presbyterian in a long line of Methodists. He lived and died in Coshocton and was an elder in the Coshocton Mill Creek organization, which was the first Presbyterian organization in the county and started at Keene. He was a builder of churches, building both the first Presbyterian and the first Methodist in Coshocton. As a young man he had built mission houses among the Wyandotte in northern Ohio. (Lawrence, 1968)

"John built the first Presbyterian Church and first Methodist Church in Coshocton and many of the small churches about the county. Staunch Presbyterian that he was, he was always a contributor to the building fund of these churches whatever the denomination." Blanche Elliott, 1941, PP, 9.

(2) 1.8b JOHN (DEACON) ELLIOTT*

(See above)

Spouse:	Nancy Jane Blyth
Birth Date:	1791/1811
Death Date:	1812/1895

Spouse Notes: Arlan Heiser (1999) has a copy of the book, "Marriages Coshocton County, Ohio 1811–1993 Volume I" and this lists the bride of John Elliott as Nancy Jane Blyth.

Second Marriage?

Marriage Date:	1812/1844

(2) 1.9a GEORGE ELLIOTT*

Birth Date:	22 Aug 1798
Birth Place:	COUNTY DONEGAL, IRELAND
Christen Place:	CAME TO AMERICA IN 1816
Death Date:	20 Feb 1875
Death Place:	MILL CREEK TWP, COSHOCTON CO, OH
Burial Place:	KEENE M.E. CEMETERY
Occupation:	FARMED & LIVED IN MILL CREEK TOWNSHIP
Religion:	Methodist, helped organize Keene Village Methodist Church

Notes: GEORGE ELLIOTT George was sixteen when he came with his mother to Doughty Creek where each purchased land. He was the son who took care of the aging parent. They lived in Mill Creek Township, Coshocton Co., Ohio, where he owned the farm with the horseshoe spring and the yard with Fannie's outdoor bake oven. (Blanche Elliott) He married a distant cousin, Mary Elliott, and later married Nancy Moore.

When the Elliotts moved from Holmes County and settled on what in later years was known as the Matt Wheatcraft farm, the son George held the title and Frances Blaine, his mother, made this her home for the rest of her life. This farm paralleled the Chestnut Ridge Road on the east side and about all that remained to identify this farm was the old church building known as Elliott's Chapel, built on the corner of George Elliott's farm in 1862. (Lawrence, 1968) The George Elliott class book of the Keene Church dated 1850 shows over half of the membership being of these three families, Elliotts, Boyds and Finlays. (Lawrence, 1968) George gave a corner of his land for a church closer to home, "Elliott Chapel". Deacon John was the carpenter in charge, which George and his neighbors provided labor. (p. 12, Blanche Elliott, 1941) The Chapel was located at the northwest corner of lot 28. The meeting house was erected in 1861, a frame building (24' x 38') and cost about $500. (p. 558 Hill, 1881).

George & Mary Elliott had several children and lost six as infants or young children. A son, James, who lived over in the Shannon valley raised several daughters. Blanche was the daughter who wrote an essay about Frances Blaine Elliott and received honorable mention in an Ohio State contest. Another daughter, Zelma collected church and family information and passed it along to her daughter, Alicia Oldham. (Lawrence, 1968)

M. Ruth Norton is a great-granddaughter of George. In 1990, Ruth was a Historian at the Roscoe Village Foundation, Coshocton, Ohio. She has access to copies of the Boyd letters (from Ohio University) which included a letter from James to Daniel & Jane Elliott Boyd (Athens County). Thomas & Lucy were mentioned in several letters from the family. They described the difficulty of raising a family in the 1840's.

Another letter (March, 1865) from Daniel Boyd to his nephew, Nathan Elliott who was serving in the Civil War, described strong Union feelings about the South. Ruth was quite sure that the "Maryann Boyd" whose name appeared on Nathan's Civil War papers was Daniel's daughter. The letters are very difficult to read because the ink has faded. They were transcribed and typed as staff at the Center found time to work on the Boyd project. George's older brother, James, wrote a letter (11 Apr 1842) to the Boyd family and said that George Elliot(t)'s daughter, Jane, had joined the Methodist Church at the beginning of the year. He described the meeting as *"Such a whillabalew(!) as we had scarsely ever seen or heard"*.

Spouse:	Mary (Cousin) ELLIOTT
Birth Date:	20 Oct 1807
Birth Place:	IRELAND
Death Date:	27 Aug 1854
Death Place:	KEENE
Education:	ELLIOTT COUSIN
Spouse Father:	ANDREW W. ELLIOTT (1772–1843)
Spouse Mother:	ELISZABETH FINLAY (1787–1861)

Spouse Notes: George and Mary (his first wife) lost 6 children as infants or young children. The children are buried in Keene Methodist Cemetery. The headstones are laid out in a row beside the large head stone of George and Mary.

Mary is identified as a "Cousin". Her parents were children of Blaine sisters. Years later, descendants searched to explain the marriage of these cousins.

Marriage Date: 23 Feb 1826

Marriage Place: HOLMS CO., ANDREW DOHERTY MG

Children: ELIZABETH CAROLINE

                      JANE

                      CHARLES

                      ALICE

                      JAMES BLAINE*

                      ANDREW C.

                      JOHN THOMAS

                      SAMUEL

                      ANN JANE

                      FANNY

                      CLARK

                      GEORGE

                      LAURA A.

                      CATHERINE (KATE)

                      MARY

Other spouses: NANCY MOORE

(3) 1.9a.1 ELIZABETH CAROLINE ELLIOTT

Birth Date: 12 Jul 1834

Death Date: Oct 1857

Notes: Elizabeth C. provided fleeting glimpse of Fannie Blaine Elliott. She described the old house in glowing terms and fond memories. (Blanche Elliott, 1941)

(3) 1.9a.2 JANE ELLIOTT

Religion: METHODIST, SPRING, 1842

(3) 1.9a.3 CHARLES ELLIOTT

Birth Date:	28 Nov 1826
Birth Place:	KEENE, COSHOCTON CO., OH
Death Date:	3 Sep 1883
Death Place:	DEFIANCE CO., OH

Notes: Source: Tom Smith Web page and file on RootsWeb.smithtm@csi.com

Spouse:	MARY JANE OVERLY
Birth Date:	Jun 1842
Birth Place:	Crawford Co., OH
Death Date:	7 Dec 1918
Death Place:	Defiance Co., OH
Burial Place:	Riverside Cemetery
Spouse Father:	George OVERLY (1819–1870)
Spouse Mother:	Hannah Hunter (1817–1898)
Marriage Date:	10 Apr 1862
Children:	HANNAH M.
	GEORGE WASHINGTON

(3) 1.9a.4 ALICE ELLIOTT

Birth Date:	5 Oct 1839
Death Date:	8 Dec 1897
Death Place:	AGE 58Y 2M 3D

| Burial Place: | KEENE, OHIO, LOWER METHODIST CEMETERY |
| Occupation: | DAUGHTER OF GEORGE & MARY ELLIOTT |

Notes: Alice was a daughter of George and Mary Elliott.

Spouse: DAVID FINDLAY?

(3) 1.9a.5 JAMES BLAINE* ELLIOTT

Birth Date:	1845
Birth Place:	FAMILY FARM NORTH OF KEENE
Christen Place:	LIVED OVER IN SHANNON VALLEY
Death Date:	20 Feb 1910
Burial Place:	KEENE, OHIO
Occupation:	FARMER
Religion:	METHODIST

Notes: James B. Elliott (1845–1910) and his wife Hester E. Elliott (1852–1926) are buried in the Methodist Cemetery in Keene, Ohio.

Spouse:	HESTER ELEANOR BOYD
Birth Date:	6 Dec 1852
Death Date:	11 Jan 1928
Burial Place:	M.E. CEMETERY, KEENE, OHIO
Occupation:	MOTHER OF 7 CHILDREN
Spouse Father:	ROBERT R. BOYD (1811–1888)
Spouse Mother:	MARY ANN JOHNSON

Spouse Notes: Burial: M.E. CEMETERY

| Marriage Date: | 27 Aug 1874 |
| Marriage Place: | COSHOCTON COUNTY, OHIO |

Children: BESSIE

               ESTELLA

               LAURA JANE*

               CHARLES BLAINE

               ZELMA ELIZABETH

               EMMA HESTER*

               ANNA BLANCHE*

(3) 1.9a.6 ANDREW C. ELLIOTT

Birth Date: 11 Feb 1828

Birth Place: KEENE, COSHOCTON CO., OH

Death Date: 15 Jul 1895

Death Place: LESTER TWP, BLACK HAWK CO., IOWA

Spouse: HANNAH WILSON

Birth Date: 14 Apr 1826

Death Date: 6 Dec 1898

Death Place: FAIRBANKS, BUCHANNAN CO., IOWA

Spouse Father: Samuel WILSON (1797–1870)

Spouse Mother: Dorcas Miller

Spouse Notes: DORCAS JANE ELLIOTT B: 1867 D: 1923 IN FAIRBANKS, BUCHANNAN CO., IO MARRIED FRANK L. ADERMAN B. ABT 1855 D:UNKNOWN IN FAIRBANKS, MARY ANN ELLIOTT B: AFTER 1857, CHARLES WILSON ELLIOTT B: AFTER 1857, ELIZABETH REBECCA ELLIOTT B: AFTER 1858, RUHMA ELLIOTT B: AFTER 1860. (Source: H. Arlan Heiser, 1997)

Marriage Date: 14 Dec 1854

Marriage Place: QUASQUETON, BUCHANNAN CO., IOWA

Children: Charles Wilson

(3) 1.9a.7 JOHN THOMAS ELLIOTT

Birth Date: 30 Jul 1829

Birth Place: OHIO

Death Date: 12 Nov 1832

Death Place: OHIO

(3) 1.9a.8 SAMUEL ELLIOTT

Birth Date: 5 Feb 1831

Death Date: 12 Nov 1832

(3) 1.9a.9 ANN JANE ELLIOTT

Birth Date: 12 Jul 1834

Death Date: Nov 1911

(3) 1.9a.10 FANNY ELLIOTT

Birth Date: 5 Oct 1837

Death Date: 15 Aug 1855

(3) 1.9a.11 CLARK ELLIOTT

Birth Date: 24 Dec 1837

Death Date: 15 Aug 1838

(3) 1.9a.12 GEORGE ELLIOTT

Birth Date:	5 Jun 1841
Birth Place:	COSHOCTON CO., OH
Death Date:	12 Jul 1893
Death Place:	BREMER, IOWA
Spouse:	RUTH ANN BECHTEL
Birth Date:	1845
Birth Place:	ABT
Death Date:	1933
Death Place:	FAIRBANK, IOWA

Spouse Notes: NATHAN ELLIOTT B: AFT 1865, GEORGE ELLIOTT, MARY ELLIOTT, ANDREW ELLIOTT. (Source: H. Arlan Heiser, 1997)

Marriage Date:	31 Oct 1865
Marriage Place:	COSHOCTON CO., OH

(3) 1.9a.13 LAURA A. ELLIOTT

Birth Date:	12 Jun 1842
Birth Place:	COSHOCTON CO., OH
Death Date:	8 Apr 1910
Death Place:	FAIRBANK, BUCHANNA CO.,IOWA

Notes: WILLIAM MILLER B: ABT 1875, JAMES MILLER B: ABT 1875, GEORGE MILLER B: ABT 1877, ANDREW MILLER B: ABT 1877, HARRY MILLER B: DEC 25, 1882 D; OCT 14, 1900 IN FAIRBANK, BUCHANNAN CO., IOWA. (Source: H. Arlan Heiser, 1997)

Spouse:	JEREMIAH A. MILLER
Birth Date:	10 Jun 1841

Death Date:	8 Dec 1910
Death Place:	FAIRBANKS, BUCHANNAN CO., IOWA
Marriage Date:	11 Dec 1870
Marriage Place:	KEENE, COSHOCTON CO., OHIO

(3) 1.9a.14 CATHERINE (KATE) ELLIOTT

Birth Date:	11 Aug 1846
Death Place:	LINCOLN, NEBRASKA
Burial Place:	Aurelia, Iowa
Spouse:	SAMUEL W. NEVILLE
Birth Date:	1845
Birth Place:	ABT
Death Place:	LINCOLN, NE
Burial Place:	AURELIA, IOWA
Occupation:	farmer
Marriage Date:	5 Mar 1883
Marriage Place:	CONSHOCTON CO., OHIO
Children:	ALLEN LESLIE

(3) 1.9a.15 MARY ELLIOTT

Birth Date:	28 Feb 1850
Death Date:	11 Aug 1917

(2) 1.9b GEORGE ELLIOTT*

(See above)

Spouse:	NANCY MOORE
Birth Date:	20 Nov 1820
Birth Place:	VA
Death Date:	21 May 1878
Death Place:	KEENE, OH

Spouse Notes: Second wife, married 2 DEC 1856, when George was 58 years old.

Marriage Date:	3 Dec 1856
Marriage Place:	COSHOCTON COUNTY, OHIO
Children:	WILLIAM
	SUSANNE
Other spouses:	Mary (Cousin) ELLIOTT

(3) 1.9b.1 WILLIAM ELLIOTT

Birth Date:	Jun 1858
Death Date:	1878
Burial Place:	Keene, OH

(3) 1.9b.2 SUSANNE ELLIOTT

Birth Date:	22 Feb 1860
Death Date:	8 Apr 1860
Burial Place:	Keene, OH

(2) 1.10 SAMUEL ELLIOTT

Birth Date:	8 May 1800
Birth Place:	CAME TO AMERICA IN 1816
Christen Place:	ASSOCATE JUDGE OF OHIO (1846–?)
Death Date:	12 Sep 1859
Death Place:	LIVED IN COSHOCTON AND DEFIANCE CO.,
Burial Place:	Independence Cemetery DOWN FROM DEFIANCE
Occupation:	FARMER, JUSTICE OF PEACE
Education:	LOST SIGHT OF ONE EYE—"SLIGHT HURT"
Religion:	METHODIST

Notes: SAMUEL ELLIOTT was a farmer, Justice of the Peace, Associate Judge, and a Methodist. For years, he lived as a neighbor to his brother, George, where Fannie made her home. His Justice of the Peace docket (1835–1845) demonstrated his fairness. He was elected an Associate Judge of Ohio and received his commission, January 10, 1846 (Blanche Elliott, 1941). He was buried at Independence, Ohio, down river from Defience. Like his siblings, he came to America in 1816.

June 16th 1842 LETTER FROM SAMUEL ELLIOTT TO DANIEL BOYD
Clary (?) township

Dear Friends (Daniel and Jane)—

I write to you to let you know how we are all in reasonable health at present thanks to God for all his mercies both g (of) a spiritual and temporal nature. Thomas and family left Roscoe about the middle (of) April having sold his premises there in view of moving to the west in company with his father-i-law (and) his wife being sick at the same time she became confined to her bed about Christmas. In March she was delivered of a man child (Thomas) which is alive and doing very well. It is with a nurse, a daughter of (?) Cuniham which lost her child. They came to our house and after suffering extremely six weeks here she died in full and certain hope of blessed immortality. She was buried on Sunday the 22nd of May in Keene her funeral was very large and a very feeling and interesting sermon was preached by the Rev. Mr. Beard of the Coshoc-

ton Circuit. He and his oldest child Simon and will remain until fall—(line illegible—Nuton (Newton) is at Alx. Finlays, Daniel at brother James, Nathan at Nephew John Elliotts. He intends to go to the West this fall and make a purchasing of land and then return and set up shop in Coshocton.

We had a stranger present itself in our family on the 10th of February which we name Nancy. I have entirely or nearly so lost the sight of my bad eye. It was ___?___ from a very slight hurt which very much ___?___me for several weeks but it is now so that it does not pain me any more. Nephew Thomas Elliott was married the to Mary Williams, daughter of Mathew Williams in the day our child was born. They have a fine boy which they name James (quicke work).

I want you to try and find where George Rickey lives in—(line illegible)—cort which will commence on the fourth of July and I would like to hear from you by that time or as soon after as you can make the necessary enquiries respecting Rickey. Will be obliqued to commence a suit against Rickey in your County if he does not comprimise if so I will pay you a visit I will not be _____to much thanks from you. Our wheats and oats crops here looks moderaly well. Corn's very backward and very much injured by the squirrals(?). Wheat is now down to seventy five cents at Roscoe and Coshocton. It rates at Massilon from ninety cents to one dollar. I took all my wheat to Massilon this last year and the greater part of the niborhood? goes there now from the advance price of wheat and the low price of goods. We do well in going. We make the trip in 2 1/2 and 3 days. We at best turn our time into money. John Boyd has rented his farm to Robert and gone to shoemaking to Keene. Andrew has sold his place for one thousand dollars and is bound for Missouri. Church matters is in a deplorable situation on this Circuit and on some of the adjoining circuits and as nigh as I can bear wherever any of the comittee(?) travels who investigated the Allan affair this—and ministray? is doing no good. How great a matter's little fire kindereth on this circuit Br—?—had to expel 10 or fifteen from the names of _____so it appears the decision of the committee have ___ ____ _____ ____was expelled for illicit connexion with his niece. He had two trials before a commitee of the most prominent members of the circuit. From his first trial he appealed to the quarterly meeting and asked his case to be remanded back to the society for a new trial which ____ was granted by the quarterly conference. He has had the second trial and verdict come(to) the same as the first (quarterly). I (hear) that he has again appealed to quarterly conference. His name is Bradley—that he would let Coshocton County know that_____Crawford and _____should not sit on Allen's trial _____ dealing has come down on his own fate however on this part of the circuit we live in peace and the preacher has had not trouble but west of Rocco and especially in the Allen nest (?) or we term it he has a hard row to hoe. Elder Powers popularity is forth (?) the decline exposity (?) among the peo-

ple there is a case of slander pending before the cort of Common Please on Mount Union between him and a Mr. McNutty representative from Knox County.—(2 lines illegible)—McNutly expects to make good his expenses—on the whole. You have done well in getting out of the bounds of the North Ohio Conference. However, I think there is a goodly number of very worthy Ministers—such as McMahon_____Linch and others. So much on the dark side of church matters but on the other side I have some news to say. In Coshocton the class numbers between 30 and 40 members and some of the richest and most influential men of the place such as of be C., Ricketts(?), Judge Schane (?) D Frew_____ Old Mr. Rickets and Mr. Thomas is there leader. They are about building a meeting house. They have 12 or 13 hundred dollars subscribed therefore aburry(?) they will succeed without doubt.

Mother's (Fannie Blaine Elliott) health is as usual. She wishes to know when you (Daniel) and Jane will be to see her and wishes to be remebered to Moses and wife and family. Sarah joins me in her respects to you. I would very much like to make you a visit this fall if we could make it at all convenient but it runs every day and will bring it. Its our trouble and Implacement(?) that we have but little time or money to spare. The Allen affair cost us one hundred dollars in a fee to Old Mr. Silliman I _____myself and Brothers for they librally helped me. I do not _____or I have any-thing more to communicate only that we_____

Samuel Elliott

Spouse:	SARAH (SALLY) SEWARD
Birth Date:	17 Nov 1804
Birth Place:	HUNTINGTON, PA
Christen Place:	George/Samuel families shared grief
Death Date:	8 Aug 1891
Death Place:	INDEPENDENCE, RICHLAND TWP, DEFIANCE CO, OHIO
Burial Place:	INDEPENDENCE, OHIO
Occupation:	MOTHER OF ONE GIRL—NANCY
Education:	WIFE OF JUDGE
Religion:	METHODIST

Spouse Notes: SARA H. SEWARD—She and Samuel buried three infants: Eleanor (1833, 3 y 8m 19d), Eliza, and Ellse (16 Aug. 1837, 1y 7m) in the Keene Methodist Cemetery. The families of George and Samuel were neighbors who rejoiced and sorrowed over their children together. Twice there were to be empty arms and aching hearts and Fannie was to see the dark hand of epidemic strike simultaneously at these two home. George lost two small sons five days apart and within a few weeks Samuel lost a small daughter; and again, George lost a year old son and Samuel lost a two year old daughter the next month. Christen: buried at least 3 infant girls in Keene

Marriage Date:	25 Oct 1825
Marriage Place:	CLARK TWP, COSHOCTON COUNTY, OHIO

Children:	ELNOR
	SIMON
	PHOBE JANE
	ELI SEWARD
	JOHN BLAINE
	ALBERT
	NANCY
	SARAH
	SAMUEL WESLEY
	HESTER ANN

(3) 1.10.1 ELNOR ELLIOTT

Birth Date:	9 May 1829
Birth Place:	KEENE TWP, COSHOCTON, OH
Death Date:	28 Jan 1833
Death Place:	KEENE, COSHOCTON CO., OH

(3) 1.10.2a SIMON ELLIOTT*

Birth Date:	8 Apr 1831
Birth Place:	KEENE TWP, COSHOCTON CO., OH
Death Date:	10 Mar 1888
Death Place:	DEFIANCE CO., OH
Spouse:	MARY ANN MASSA
Birth Date:	2 Apr 1836
Death Date:	1915
Death Place:	KEENE, OH
Other spouses:	MARY JANE LANGLEY

(3) 1.10.2b SIMON ELLIOTT*

(See above)

Spouse:	MARY JANE LANGLEY
Birth Date:	26 Nov 1825
Death Date:	29 Feb 1872
Marriage Date:	16 Apr 1854
Marriage Place:	COSHOCTON CO., OH
Other spouses:	MARY ANN MASSA

(3) 1.10.3 PHOBE JANE ELLIOTT

Birth Date:	26 May 1833
Birth Place:	KEENE TWP, COSHOCTON CO., OH
Death Date:	25 Sep 1903
Death Place:	OKOLONA, DEFIANCE CO.,OH

Spouse:	JOHN B. YAUNT
Birth Date:	1830
Birth Place:	ABT IN VA
Death Date:	27 Apr 1901
Death Place:	DEFIANCE CO., OH

(3) 1.10.4 ELI SEWARD ELLIOTT

Birth Date:	27 Dec 1835
Birth Place:	KEENE TWP COSHOCTON CO., OH
Death Date:	16 Aug 1837
Death Place:	KEENE TWP COSHOCTON CO., OH

(3) 1.10.5 JOHN BLAINE ELLIOTT

Birth Date:	5 Dec 1837
Birth Place:	KEENE TWP, COSHOCTON CO., OH
Death Date:	14 Jul 1892
Death Place:	INDEPENDENC, DIFIANCE CO., OH
Spouse:	HENRIETTA MIRANDA DODD
Birth Date:	12 Mar 1843
Birth Place:	WADSWORTH (?)
Death Place:	INDEPENDENCE, DEFIANCE CO., OH
Occupation:	MOTHER OF 8 CHILDREN

Spouse Notes:
NETTIE, EMMA, SARAH, WILLIAM F., RUTH, RACHEL, ELLEN, CHARLES

Marriage Date: 8 Sep 1861

Marriage Place: DEFIANCE CO., OH

(3) 1.10.6 ALBERT ELLIOTT

Birth Date: 27 Dec 1839

Birth Place: KENNE TWP, COSHOCTON CO., OH

Death Date: 31 Aug 1913

Death Place: INDEPENDENCE, DEFIANCE CO., OH

Spouse: HENRIETTE EMERY

Birth Date: 22 Apr 1833

Birth Place: WADSWORTH, OH

Death Date: 15 Dec 1911

Death Place: INDEPENDENCE, DEFIANCE CO., OH

Spouse Notes: SAMUEL EMERY, FLORA BELLE, ALBERT WOLCUTT

Marriage Date: 22 Sep 1868

(3) 1.10.7 NANCY ELLIOTT

Birth Date: 10 Feb 1842

Birth Place: KEENE TWP COSHOCTON, OH

Death Date: 17 Apr 1900

Death Place: INDEPENDENCE, DEFIANCE CO., OH

Spouse: JACOB YOUNG

Birth Date: 2 Jun 1833

Birth Place: ST. MARIE OF THE MINES, FRANCE

Death Date:	23 Jan 1923
Death Place:	INDEPENDENCE, DEFIANCE CO., OH
Marriage Date:	6 Nov 1866
Children:	PHILLIP
	GUESTAVE ELLIOTT
	JOSEPHINE
	CHARLES ELLIOTT
	MARY ELIZABETH
	ANNA
	JOHN JACOB

(3) 1.10.8 SARAH ELLIOTT

Birth Date:	26 Oct 1843
Birth Place:	KEENE TWP, COSHOCTON CO., OH
Death Date:	12 Apr 1902
Death Place:	DETROIT, MI

Notes: EMMA, SIMON

Spouse:	ADOLPHUS CURRY
Birth Date:	1840
Death Date:	Nov 1869

(3) 1.10.9 SAMUEL WESLEY ELLIOTT

Birth Date:	19 Dec 1845
Birth Place:	KEENE TWP, COSHOCTON CO., OH
Death Date:	Dec 1917
Death Place:	SANDUSKY OHIO SOLDIERS HOME

(3) 1.10.10 HESTER ANN ELLIOTT

Birth Date:	5 Oct 1848
Birth Place:	KEENE TWP, COSHOCTON CO., OH
Death Date:	2 Mar 1920
Death Place:	AYERSVILLE, DEFIANCE CO.,OH
Spouse:	JOHN MEYERS
Birth Date:	1845
Marriage Date:	9 Feb 1868

(2) 1.11 ANNE ELLIOTT

Birth Date:	17 May 1802
Birth Place:	IRELAND
Christen Place:	CAME TO AMERICA IN 1816
Death Date:	16 Aug 1825
Burial Place:	BURIED IN/NEAR DELAWARE, OHIO
Occupation:	died leaving her first born infant

Notes: Anne married and lived near Delaware, Ohio, until her early death (Blanche Elliott Essay, 1941). She died leaving a first born infant.

Spouse:	LYMAN SHAFFER
Birth Date:	7 Oct 1800
Death Date:	15 Nov 1871
Occupation:	TANNER/FARMER
Religion:	Methodist

Spouse Notes: Lyman Shafer (1830 Census) Holmes Co., Hardy Township, page 288, Milesburg. Lyman bought land from Thomas Elliott (Lot 66) in Millersburg in 1830. He and Margaret sold this lot in 1835. There was not "Jayson/

Jason" in the Holmes Co. Deed Index. (Source: JHScottie@aol.com, Jane to Sandra Yragcurt@aol.com in a note regarding the Shaffer/Elliott connection dated 4/4/00)

Marriage Date: 8 May 1823

(2) 1.12 JANE ELLIOTT

Birth Date:	8 Apr 1803
Birth Place:	CAME TO AMERICA IN 1816
Christen Place:	LIVED IN COSHOCTON & ATHENS CO.
Death Date:	4 Oct 1886
Death Place:	NEAR ATHENS CO. LINE (COOLVILLE) MEIGS CO.
Burial Place:	BURIED IN TUPPERS PLAINS, MEIGS CO.
Occupation:	HOME MAKER & MOTHER OF 9 CHILDREN
Education:	HOUSEWIFE, MOTHER &
Religion:	METHODIST

Notes: JANE ELLIOTT BOYD. Jane lived in Coshocton County and Athens County. She married her Irish sweetheart who followed her to Ohio with his family. They raised a family of 9 children. She was buried in Tuppers Plains Cemetery, Meigs County, near the Athens County line. Like her sibling, she came to America in 1816 with Fanny Blaine Elliott. "One of her children, Margaret, (known lovingly as Maggie) was the first woman graduate (1873) at Ohio University." (Source: Blanche Elliott, 1941, pp.9). Ohio University built a woman's hall in 1913, and named it Margaret Boyd Hall. The Methodist Cemetery in Tuppers Plains lies on the west side of the highway was you enter the village from the north. The church building was gone (1993) and the yard converted to business use. The cemetery appeared to be maintained only occasionally, and lay only partly visible from the highway. In the near side of the cemetery, the Boyd monuments were augmented by headstones for each grave. The main monument is cracked near the top. It has a basic information message about father Daniel, son John and daughter Mary Ann.
Burial: METHODIST CHURCH CEMETERY

Spouse:	DANIEL BOYD
Birth Date:	7 Sep 1794
Birth Place:	DONEGEL, IRELAND
Christen Place:	moved to Athens County, Ohio
Death Date:	20 Aug 1867
Death Place:	FARM NEAR COOLVILLE, OHIO
Burial Place:	BURIED IN TUPPERS PLAINS, MEIGS CO.
Occupation:	WEAVER/FARMER
Education:	BELIEVED IN HIGHER EDUCATION
Religion:	METHODIST
Spouse Father:	ROBERT ALBERT BOYD (1760–1836)
Spouse Mother:	JANE RAMSEY (1760–1826)

Spouse Notes: DANIEL BOYD. Daniel married Jane Elliott in 1825. He was living with his father, Robert, east of Keene which older folks of the 1960's generation knew as the Everett Boyd farm. Daniel came to America a year or more before his family, knowing that he would find his childhood sweetheart here in the 'Garden of Eden.' Daniel and Jane Elliott Boyd bought the farm just below Keene which included all of the south part of the village and the original church site for the first Methodist church building. Court house records at Coshocton show the church deed written in 'goose quill' longhand from the Boyds to the Methodist Church in 1835, two acres for $50. A history of Keene states that Daniel Boyd had a pet deer which followed him like a dog and would be seen at the store, which Richard, Daniel's brother-in-law, kept in the old Charlie Brenly house at the southwest corner of the cemetery. This was the first store in Keene. Daniel Boyd believed strongly in higher education so they did not stay long enough at Keene to see the first church built but moved down near Athens where eventually Margaret Boyd (1873) became the first woman to graduate from Ohio University, and Boyd Hall was named for her. Daniel himself, when he lived at Keene, took a special course in Latin, walking back and forth to Coshocton each day. (Lawrence, 1968)

LETTER WRITTEN BY D. BOYD, BUT PROBABLY NOT SENT TO NEPHEW, NATHAN ELLIOTT.

Coolville March 28th 1865

Dear Nathan,

This is a wet day and I will write you a few lines myself. We received two letters from you yesterday, one to Mary Ann and one to Margaret. You say you are afraid you will never see the union as it was. Do not be discouraged. The union will be preserved and I hope you will live to see it done, and that you will have the honor of helping to do it. We had a letter from Johnson Boyd and one from George Boyd both yesterday. We were glad to hear that our relatives in the Army are all living and feel to thank Providence for their preservation so far and trust that they will be spared to the end of this wicked rebellion and return to their respective homes in safety. From some of your letters I was afraid your mind was getting bewildered on the subject of the war and the design of the emancipation proclamation. You seemed to think you were fighting to free slaves; that was a great mistake. Your business is to save the Union and let slavery take care of itself. And who is so blind as not to see that slavery was the great strength of the rebels and anything the government could do to weaken the rebellion was perfectly right and what business has a soldier to enquire whether a negro is better in a state of slavery or a state of freedom. It is strange indeed to hear of any one preferring to have negroes raising corn and pork for rebels while rebels are shooting down union men and striving to destroy the best government in the world. Again it is said you have turned democrat. Well, I have no objection to that if it be of the true Jefferson stamp, but if it is of that kind who sympathizes with rebels and do all they can to throw obstacles in the way of government I pity you. But I hope better things of you, and again there will be, or is now, union men. The balance of them will be butternuts or copperheads, and will be reckoned in the same category as Burr and Arnold, and I believe their children after them will share the disgrace of sympathizing with treason. And again, much as I long for your safe return and you have my poor prayers every day that God would preserve you yet I would rather hear of your bones bleaching on a southern battlefield than you to come home disgraced from the Army. But enough on this subject. Now for the news. A few deserters in Noble County and their Butternut friends said they would not return to the army and they would not be taken. One of the letters sent to the army encouraging desertion fell into the hands of a colonel. This was sent to governor Todd who ordered the arrest of the deserters. But the Copperheads to the number of 200 armed to resist. The Corporal and his men retired without giv-

ing all the details. Marshal Sands returned in a few days with two hundred armed soldiers and some mounted volunteers. The Butternuts got scared and by last accounts fourteen of the insurgents was arrested and doubtless will be dealt with according to their crimes. Fanny and Mag have written to you and I need not repeat what they have said. If I knowed you cared about papers I would send one occasionally. When you write tell us all you know of our friends in the army. Do you know anything of Andrew Duncan. Give my respects to Jeffers boys and D. Noyes, and again pray be hopeful and trustful and may the blessing of God be upon you. Respectfully,

Your Uncle Daniel Boyd

Daniel Boyd was born in Ireland in 1794, emigrated to the United States in 1819 and settled in Carthage Township as a farmer in 1838. He was an active member of the Methodist Church and an excellent citizen. He died Aug 20, 1867. His oldest son, Dr John E. Boyd, died in West Virginia in 1855. His other two sons, Hugh and William F., graduated at the Ohio University in 1860 and 1866 respectively, and have engaged successfully in teaching. (Walker, History of Athens County, 1869, pp. 458) Carthage township lies just west of Troy Township, and the village of Coolville, Ohio.

Marriage Date:	8 Nov 1825
Marriage Place:	AT HOME, Doughty Creek, COSHOCTON (HOLMES) COUNTY
Children:	JOHN ELLIOTT
	MARY ANN
	JANE
	KATHRYN
	HUGH
	LUCY A.
	WILLIAM FLETCHER
	FANNY BLAINE
	MARGARET "MAGGIE"

(3) 1.12.1 JOHN ELLIOTT BOYD

Birth Date:	1 Sep 1826
Birth Place:	KEENE, OHIO
Death Date:	22 May 1855
Death Place:	WEST VIRGINIA
Burial Date:	SeeNotes
Burial Place:	TUPPERS PLAINS, OHIO
Occupation:	DR.
Education:	OHIO UNIVERSITY
Religion:	METHODIST
Spouse:	CAROLINE CARR
Marriage Date:	22 Jun 1853
Children:	JANE ELLIOTT "Ella"

(3) 1.12.2 MARY ANN BOYD

Birth Date:	7 Oct 1828
Birth Place:	KEENE, COSHOCTON, OHIO
Christen Place:	DID BEAUTIFUL NEEDLE WORK
Death Date:	30 Aug 1867
Burial Place:	TUPPERS PLAINS, MEIGS COUNTY, OHIO
Occupation:	TAUGHT SCHOOL IN KEENE, OHIO, 1849
Education:	ONE ROOM SCHOOL TEACHER
Religion:	METHODIST

Notes: Mary Ann Boyd was the second child of Daniel and Jane Elliott Boyd, born October 7, 1828, died August 30, 1867. She was a teacher in Coshocton County, Ohio., married and did beautiful needle work. She was buried in the Methodist Church yard, Tuppers Plains, Meigs County, Ohio. (Source: One

Hundred Years in America, pp. 12) She lies buried in the Methodist Church yard next to her parents and brother John. She died within a week of her father's death. (Aug 30, 1867 vs Aug 20, 1867). The Church building was abandoned in the 1930's and the graves are located behind a storage shed and business out of sight of the road passing through the village. (The burial yard lies on the east side of the village on the north side of the road.)

23 mar 1849—LETTER FROM MARYANN BOYD TO HER MOTHER AND FATHER (DANIEL AND JANE)

Keene, March 23th 1849

Dear Mother

For the first time I take my pen to write a few lines to you feeling that it is a hard way to talk to you and yet glad that I can speak this way to you. Two weeks ago today—the next Friday after school was out Elizabeth Elliott brought a horse to Keene for me so I went home with her. The next Monday Ann, Jane and I went to see Aunt Fanny. We found her and her family all well. Moses and Edward (Elliott) will start for the Maumee in a week or two with Charles Elliott. I stayed a night at Uncle Samuels and one at Alexander Finley. Nansyes has not of very good health but she is merry enought. The next Friday Elizabeth and I went to see Uncle James. The first thing I got was a good kiss and the next then a pinch of snuff, he has been quite unwell but is now much better. Aunt Hester is in a bad condition indeed. She can get from the bed to the fire, and don't leave her bedroom at all, she says she feels a great deal of pain. The United Brethern have been holding a big Meeting up there they had great times, such shouting and jumping as you know they sometimes have, and Moses got religion, but I won't say any more about it for Uncle James said he would write to Father and tell all about it but as Uncle Georges folks are very busy with their horses we had to come back the next day so I had no chance of visiting any in that part of the country but when we were coming back we called on Mary Graham. She was very glad to see me and would not let us off without supper, she looks very natural. So Sunday I came back to Keene and call this home at present. Uncle Simon (1809–1849) has been out here this week. He stayed two nights and (went) back, I did not see him. He say Aunt Christiani has very poor health. Uncle Thomas had the California fever and was going to start for that country but Uncle George and Samuel heard of it and went to see him. He said his wife could take care of the children but they persuarded him to stay at home, so he says no more about it. Aunt Maryann in Keene has had the tooth-

ache almost all winter. She first took cold and it settled in her head. I got up in the mornings and had breakfast ready before Aunt or Uncle were all ready for it. Uncle Wm. Boyd has bought the Wilkison farm so you see he is going ahead. Daniel Boyds is about as usual. Marty and Mary are doing very well in Coshocton. William Walker is talking of going to Uncle John Elliott to learn the carpenter traid (trade). Some of his friends want him to go farming but he has so many advisors it is hard for him to know what to do. They are living with the Judge (Samuel Elliott), (his daughter) Mary's health is not very good. As you said if I could get a school here I might stay all summer so Uncle Robert (Robert R. Boyd 1811–1888) got me the school in his district. I get 20 dollars for the Quarter have no writings drew yet but I will have to go to town for a certificate as soon as I can. It will commense on the second Monday in April. Father said in his last letter that he wanted me to write every month whether I get one or not and certainly if you expect me to write every month between you all you can write every month so I will inspect (expect) one. I think Jane and Catharine might wright (write), it is now a long time since I heard from you so if you have not wrote lately I hope you will very soon. Uncle Richard says there is a letter in the post office from Coolville for Wm. Boyd. I suppose it is from some of you. Enought of news for this time, but my own health is very good. The headache troubled me but very little. Remember your distant daughter although with the kindest of friends a daughter from home.

Yours afectionately, Maryann Boyd

P.S. March 26ᵗʰ this morning at 8 o'clock I started to Coshocton with Uncle Samuel to get my certificate. I got through_____so now I am ready for my school. I will post my letter today. Ms Boyd

COPIED FROM ORIGINAL LETTER BY RUTH NORTON, ROSCOE VILLAGE FOUNDATION, 7/91.

Spouse: WILLIAM JOHNSTON

Marriage Date: 29 May 1855

Marriage Place: COSHOCTON COUNTY, OHIO

(3) 1.12.3 JANE BOYD

Birth Date:	5 Jan 1831
Death Date:	11 Oct 1885
Burial Place:	TUPPER SPRINGS, MEIGS COUNTY, OHIO
Occupation:	TEACHER AND HOME MAKER AFTER 1855

Notes: Burial: TUPPER SPRINGS, MEIGS COUNTY, OHIO

(3) 1.12.4 KATHRYN BOYD

Birth Date:	22 Mar 1833
Death Date:	1913
Burial Place:	ATHENS, OHIO
Occupation:	TEACHER IN COUNTY & HIGH SCHOOL(40 YRS)

(3) 1.12.5a HUGH BOYD*

Birth Date:	6 Aug 1835
Birth Place:	14
Death Date:	7 Mar 1917
Death Place:	Mount Vernon, Linn Co., IO
Burial Place:	MT. VERNON, IOWA
Occupation:	TEACHER, MINISTER, PROF. OF LATIN (40YRS)
Education:	OHIO UNIVERSITY, GRAD.1860, College professor in Iowa
Religion:	METHODIST

Notes: Hugh Boyd, fifth child of Daniel and Jane Elliott Boyd, born August 6, 1835; died 1917; buried at Mt. Vernon, Iowa. He was a teacher, minister and Professor of Latin for forty years at Cornell College, Mt. Vernon, Iowa. He was married to Ida Patterson. To this union two children were born, Luella Boyd, home at Mr. Vernon, Iowa, and Robert Boyd, deceased. After the death of his first wife he married Mary Moody in 1874. To this union four children were born, Granville Moody Boyd, who died in infancy; Clifford Moody Boyd, Lucy Moody Boyd, and Elizabeth, who died in infancy. (Source: One Hundred Years in America, pp. 12)

Spouse:	IDA PATTERSON
Birth Date:	25 Mar 1839
Death Date:	21 Oct 1867[15]
Occupation:	Housewife
Marriage Date:	21 Aug 1860[13]
Marriage Place:	Amesville, Athens Co. OH
Children:	Luella
	Robert Allyn
Other spouses:	Ellen Moody

(3) 1.12.5b HUGH BOYD*

(See above)

Spouse:	Ellen Moody
Children:	Granville Moody
	Clifford Moody
	Lucy Moody
	Elizabeth
Other spouses:	IDA PATTERSON

(3) 1.12.6 LUCY A. BOYD

Birth Date:	5 Sep 1837
Death Date:	1912

Burial Place:	ATHENS COUNTY
Occupation:	TEACHER

(3) 1.12.7 WILLIAM FLETCHER BOYD

Birth Date:	15 Feb 1840
Death Date:	21 Jun 1911
Death Place:	CINCINNATI, OHIO
Occupation:	LAWYER (BOYCE&BOYD-CINCINNATI)
Education:	OHIO UNIVERSITY, 1866
Religion:	METHODIST
Spouse:	ALICE WOOD
Marriage Date:	12 Jun 1883

(3) 1.12.8 FANNY BLAINE BOYD

Birth Date:	6 Sep 1842
Birth Place:	Carthage Twp., Athens Co., OH
Death Date:	1899
Death Place:	ATHENS, OHIO
Burial Place:	ATHENS, OHIO
Spouse:	CHARLES W. LAWRENCE
Birth Date:	1 Jul 1840
Birth Place:	Carthage Twp., Athens Co., OH
Death Date:	1919
Death Place:	abt in Athens, Athens Co., OH
Marriage Date:	16 Aug 1865
Marriage Place:	Athens, OH

Children: WESLEY BOYD

                   PEARLY BOYD

(3) 1.12.9 MARGARET "MAGGIE" BOYD

Birth Date: 7 Apr 1845

Death Date: 10 Oct 1905

Death Place: CINCINNATI, OHIO

Occupation: TEACHER

Education: 1876–1ST WOMAN GRADUATE—OHIO UNIV.

Religion: METHODIST

Notes: Margaret, (known lovingly as Maggie) was the first woman graduate (1873) at Ohio University." (Blanche Elliott, 1941, pp.9) Ohio University constructed a woman's hall in 1913, and named it Margaret Boyd Hall.

Spouse: L. K. ROBERTSON

Marriage Date: 16 Sep 1880

Marriage Place: COSHOCTON COUNTY, OHIO

(2) 1.13 NANCY ELLIOTT

Birth Date: 7 May 1805

Birth Place: CAME TO AMERICA IN 1816

Notes: Nothing is known of Nancy (Blanche Elliott, 1941)

Spouse: JAYSON SHAFER

Birth Date: 1805

Spouse Notes: Jane (JHScottie@aol.com) wrote to Sandra (Yragcurt@aol.com) wonders about the Blanche Elliott Essay information regarding Ann and Nancy. "I never have seen a "Janson" Shafer/Shaffer—and wonder if this may have been a misreading of "Lyman" in one of its many misspellings. Often "L" is mistaken for "S" or "J" or "I"—and I think that might be the case here. And County Clerks are notoriously bad spellers and penmen! Marriage records indicate that Nancy married Lyman Shaffer.

(2) 1.14a THOMAS ELLIOTT*

Birth Date:	6 Aug 1807
Birth Place:	ARDARA, KILLIBEGS, DONEGAL, IRELAND
Christen Place:	LIVED IN MILLERSBURG, OH, IL, & KS
Death Date:	1879 or Later
Death Place:	LAST HEARD FROM COWLEY, KS. (1875), RETURNED TO DAWSON, IL
Burial Place:	(Vol 611, p. 24) 1875 KANSAS CENSUS
Occupation:	WHEEL WRIGHT, CARPENTER, AS'ST MINISTER
Education:	PRIMARY EDUCATION IN IRELAND
Religion:	METHODIST

Notes: THOMAS ELLIOTT. Thomas came to Ohio with his family as a young boy (age 9). The family landed in the Inner Harbor, Baltimore, MD. They purchased a team and wagon to walk the National Road during the summer and fall of 1816. The wooden shipping box that carried most of Thomas' goods was handed down through the generations to Virginia Stevens. She wrote (9/90) that she has an immigrants chest that the Elliott family brought over from Europe. It is something to see! 2 ft wide, 4 ft long and about 3 ft high. Her Mom always cherished that chest. Big metal handles on each end. The family prided their walk to Ohio by saying they forded every stream on the way without help, except for the float across the Ohio river. Frances Blaine Elliott led 9 of her children to land purchased in Mill Creek Township (organized in 1817) where the Elliott family lived when first they arrived in Ohio. Near them, Solomon Vail opened the first corn-grinding mill. The mill was enlarged a few years later (1831) and Thomas Elliott brought the stones for the mill from Mansfield. He was rewarded with a pair of wedding shoes fashioned by Mr. Vail who was a 'jack of all trades'. In early 1832, Thomas and Lucy were married and lived in Millersburg near her parents, Their first child, Simon, was born Dec. 15, 1832. "George, Samuel,

Thomas, Jane and their neighbors were the first members of the Keene village M.E. church five miles from George's home. They met in each other's homes, of course, that meant Fannie's home, too, where they shouted and sang and prayed and wept for joy till the wall of the homes must have fairly buckled with the hallelujah shouts of redemption or...shuddered with the wailing of fire and brimstone threats." (Blanche Elliott, 1941, pp. 11.) In 1832, Thomas applied for U.S. citizenship in the Holmes County Courthouse. He was sworn as a naturalized citizen, October 15, 1835. (Dates from original records, Vol. 2, 1835, Probate Records, Court House, Millersburg, Ohio.)

By 1841, Thomas had moved to Roscoe, across the Muskingum River from Coshocton, where Nathan Saunders, their fourth child, was born. (Based on information from an application for veteran benefits completed by Nathan in 1910). The child was named for his maternal grandfather whom Thomas greatly admired. Nathan Saunders planned to go west to Oregon or California in the next year or two. Thomas sold his lot and barn (Millersburg) in the spring of 1842, as he planned to go west with the Saunders family. (See the Boyd letters) Other children included Daniel Gross (1834–1912), Newton (1839–1843), Nathan (1841–1915), and Thomas (1842–1899). Newton died as a young child (1843) probably from the lung fever. Lucy died as a result of childbirth complications and winter fever following the birth of Thomas (1842). (See Boyd letters for Jame's & Samuel's letters on Thomas, Lucy & their children). She was buried in the Keene Methodist Lower Cemetery. Thomas's plans to go west were shattered. Perhaps their stepmother, Nancy Nutt Elliott, raised the boys. However, the Boyd letters suggest the children were raised by other family members, at least for a while. For example, Daniel Boyd married Jane Elliott in 1825 and his Aunt and her family in Coolville, Ohio raised likely Nathan. Thomas married Nancy Nutt in Coshocton in 1844. Their marriage is recorded in Coshocton public records. The marriage produced four more children: Charles H., David S., Napoleon B. and Lucy. In 1849, Maryann Boyd wrote in a letter to her mother and father that Uncle Thomas had the California fever and was going to start for that country but Uncle George and Samuel heard of it and went to see him. Thomas said his wife could take care of the children but they persuaded him to stay at home, so he says no more about it. Thomas stayed in Coshocton County for the next 20 years. In 1870, the Methodist Church in Kansas needed an assistant pastor and Thomas volunteered to go to Guilford, Kansas in order to work on the construction of a Methodist church building in this new village. People were moving to Kansas, buying land for farming, railroads were expanding and constructing tracks where villages were forming. In 1871, a Methodist circuit in Central Kansas was divided, part retained the name of Fredonia, while part became New Albany. (Schools, Churches, Societies in the History of the State of Kansas by A.T. Andreas, 1883.)

In addition, a newspaper, Guilford Citizen, began operating in Guilford, Kansas from April 21, 1870 until it moved to Neodasha and became the Wilson County Citizen. At most, Guilford was a mere hamlet of ten or a dozen houses, that expected to be the county seat. When the location of government was established in Fredonia, the hamlet quietly disappeared.

According to the 1870 Kansas Census, Thomas Elliott lived near what became the town of Fredonia, Wilson County, Kansas. He was listed as age 63, with real estate of $500, personal property of $100, born in Ireland and parents of foreign birth. For a time, he lived in Guilford, a small hamlet on the Missouri Pacific railroad, along the Verdigris river, north of Neodesha, North East of Fredonia and South East of Benedict. No visible trace of the hamlet exists today. In 1870, Thomas was a pioneer who helped settle Kansas. He was the asst. Pastor, Methodist Church, sponsored by his congregation in Illinois, to help build a church building in Guilford. Town leaders expected the county seat to be located in the geographic center of the county, but it never happened quite that way. The completed building was used as a school for many years, and finally taken down in the early '20s. "Rev. Elliot is getting the material on the ground for a large business house, to be erected on State Street, nearly opposite Morse's store." (Guilford Citizen, May 28, 1870) "Rev. Thomas Elliott, who is superintending the building of the M.E. Church at this place, and who is the chief architect, is progressing finely, and will soon have the body of it up." (Guilford Citizen, Aug 20, 1870)[51] In 1874, Thomas wrote to his older brother George who was living in Coshocton County that his second wife, Nancy thought that he was partial to first wife, Lucy's, children. She felt her children were being left out. The Kansas Census of 1875 listed Thomas Elliott as age 68, occupation wagon maker, born in Ireland, where from to Kansas was Illinois, living in Cowley, Wilson County, in the township of Verdigris (Vol. 611, p. 24) After 1875, his where abouts is a calculated guess. He could have lived near one of the children, possibly, Charles H. (1845–1931) who moved to Sangamon County, Ilinois, from Ohio at age 9 and lived there until he moved to Kansas. Charles homesteaded in Neosho County in the early 1870's, then moved to Greenwood County, and several years later (1884) to Cowley County. However, Thomas probably returned to Illinois.

Saunders family records indicate Thomas died in Sangamon Co., Illinois, and is buried somewhere around Dawson, Illinois.

Spouse:	LUCY W. SAUNDERS
Birth Date:	1812
Birth Place:	R.I.
Death Date:	18 May 1842
Death Place:	SAM ELLIOTT'S, CLARY TOWNSHIP
Burial Date:	20 May 1842
Burial Place:	METHODIST CHURCH, KEENE, OHIO (LOWER)
Occupation:	HOMEMAKER & MOTHER OF FIVE
Religion:	METHODIST
Spouse Father:	NATHAN SAUNDERS II (1785–1854)
Spouse Mother:	MARY ROSS (1788–1870)

Spouse Notes: LUCY W_____. SAUNDERS. Letters written between Elliott and Boyd families provide the basis for most of what is known about the Saunders family. Thomas met and married Lucy, 9 JAN 1832 near Millersburg, Ohio. In 1832, they lived in Millersburg and their first child, Simon was born Dec. 15, 1832. Other children included Daniel Gross (1834–1912), Newton (1839–1843), Nathan (1841–1915), and Thomas (1842–1899). Newton died as a young child (1843) probably of the same childhood disease that took his mother the year before. Lucy died (20 MAY 1842) after a six weeks illness as a result of "Lung Fever" complications following the birth of Thomas.

James Elliott wrote to the Boyd family (letter dated 11th April 1842) indicating that:
"All our Families now are in tolerable good health except my Brother Thomas' Family. Lucy has been confined to her bed these many months but she has recovered so far that she bore to be removed to my Brother Sam's on last Friday and it was a great undertaking. She has had another boy (Thomas) about two weeks ago and considering her weak helpless condition the child seems to do well. Her mother has taken the baby and the other two youngest children (Nathan and Thomas) home and the two oldest (Simon and Daniel) is with us (James Elliott). Tom has sold his barn and lot for 800 dollars and his Father in Law has also sold and they all mean to start for the Ioway

territory as soon as their health will permit which will be some time as Tom and all the Family was all so bad about a month ago that one could not give the other a drink but they are recovering fast. A great many has died with a complaint they call Lung Fever and the Scarlet Fever has also carried away a great many children and grown people."

Another letter to the Boyd family quoted Samuel Elliott: (letter dated June 16th 1842)

"Thomas and family left Roscoe about the middle (of) April having sold his premises there in view of moving to the west in company with his father-i-law (and) his wife being sick at the same time she became confined to her bed about Christmas. In March she was delivered of a man child (Thomas) which is alive and doing very well. It is with a nurse, a daughter of (?) Cuniham which lost her child. Samuel wrote they came to our house and after suffering extremely six weeks here she died in full and certain hope of blessed immortality. She was buried on Sunday the 22nd of May in Keene. Her funeral was very large and a very feeling and interesting sermon was preached by the Rev. Mr. Beard of the Coshocton Circuit. Thomas and his oldest child Simon and will remain until fall—(line illegible—Nuton (Newton) is at Alx. Finlays, Daniel at brother James, and Nathan at Nephew John Elliotts. Thomas intends to go to the West this fall and make a purchasing of land and then return and set up shop in Coshocton."

In still another letter (23 mar 1849), Maryann Boyd wrote to her parents that:

"Thomas had the California fever and was going to start for that country but Uncle George and Samuel heard of it and went to see him. Thomas said his wife could take care of the children but they persuaded him to stay at home, so he says no more about it."

The boys were probably raised by their stepmother, Nancy Nutt Elliott or by members of their extended family.

Marriage Date:	9 Jan 1832
Marriage Place:	HOLMES COUNTY, OHIO by S. Ruark, M.G.
Children:	SIMON
	DANIEL GROSS
	NEWTON

NATHAN SAUNDERS

THOMAS

Other spouses: NANCY NUTT

(3) 1.14a.1 SIMON ELLIOTT

Birth Date:	15 Dec 1832
Birth Place:	MILLERSBURG, OHIO
Christen Place:	RETURNED TO OHIO AFTER 14 YRS IN KANSAS
Death Place:	JEFFERSON TOWNSHIP
Burial Place:	VILLAGE OF WARSAW, OHIO
Occupation:	FARMER & MOULDER (FOUNDRY)
Education:	attended school to age 16 in MILLERSBURG, OHIO
Religion:	MISSIONARY, INDIAN RESERVATION IN KANS

SIMON ELLIOTT—Simon was the oldest of 5 boys. He was named for his Uncle Simon, younger brother of Thomas. He was born in Millersburg, Holmes County, Ohio, December 15, 1832. Until about the age of sixteen he attended school and worked with his father in the wagon shop. He then began the molder's trade in the foundry at Roscoe, and remained there about two years. He went to Walhonding in 1848, remained until the year 1864, and the next spring went to Kansas, where he followed farming. About 1865, he lived near Wetmore, Kansas, on the Potowatomie Indian Reservation. Until about the age of 16, he attended school and worked in his father's wagon shop. He learned the molder's trade in Roscoe, moved to Walhonding, where he met his wife and remained there until 1864. They moved to Kansas in 1865. They had one son, Edward L., born 25 August 1866. They farmed for 14 years, and returned home because of his wife's ill health. He returned to Coshocton County, Jefferson Township, where he died and was buried. (pp 674, History of Coshocton County, Biographical Sketches, 1881) In 1875–77, Simon operated a foundry on the basement floor of a three-story general repair shop to the right of the Walhonding bridge in the village of Warsaw (pp 519–520)

Spouse:	ELECTRA BUTLER
Birth Date:	1835
Birth Place:	OHIO
Christen Place:	RETURNED HOME IN 1874
Death Date:	1875
Death Place:	WARSAW, JEFFERSON TOWNSHIP
Burial Place:	JEFFERSON TOWNSHIP
Occupation:	HOUSEWIFE, ONE SON
Religion:	METHODIST

Spouse Notes: Electra was the daughter of Allen and Margaret (Smith) Butler. Their son, Edward L. was born, August 25, 1866, in the Osage Indian Reserve, in Kansas. (Pp 674, History of Coshocton County, Biographical Sketches, 1881)

Marriage Date:	3 Oct 1857
Marriage Place:	WALHONDING, OHIO
Children:	EDWARD L.

(3) 1.14a.2 DANIEL GROSS ELLIOTT

Birth Date:	21 Sep 1834
Birth Place:	Holmes Co., OHIO
Death Date:	20 Feb 1912
Death Place:	HOUSTON, MO.
Burial Place:	Pine Lawn Cem., Houston, MO
Occupation:	JOURNEYMAN, CIVIL WAR VETERAN, FARMER, MECHANIC
Religion:	METHODIST

Notes: DANIEL GROSS ELLIOTT was the second born (21 SEP 1834) of five boys of Thomas & Lucy Saunders Elliott. When Daniel's mother died, the older boys, Simon and Daniel went to live with George or James Elliott. Daniel must have been on his own by the time he was 16 years old (1854). Daniel married Catherine Henderson in 1855. He was drafted for military service during the Civil War in 1862. His complexion was florid, eyes gray, hair red, and by occupation a machinist. He was 5 ft. 9 1/2 in tall and 28 years old when he reported to Camp Zanesville, Ohio, Sep. 1, 1862. The bounty paid for his enlistment was $25 dollars and a premium of $2. When he joined for duty for three years, he was appointed Corporal. August 5, at Walhonding, Ohio, and promoted 4Sergt. (Dec 26, 1862) Co. H., 97th Reg't Ohio Infantry. He was issued one haversack and 1 canteen (Sept. 1863), and ordered to Columbus, Ohio, after drafted men by Major Ben. Thomas. He was on detached duty for recruiting service, Army of the Cumberland, headquarters, per S.F.O. 48, dated Feb. 17, 1864. He was mustered out in compliance with a telegram from the War Dept., dated May 18/29, 1865. (mustered out on individual roll June 15, 1865). He was a patient on the Hospital Muster Roll, No. 8, U.S.A. General Hospital, Nashville, Tenn., in July and August 1864. He was reported present and died Sep. 6., 1864., according to J. Castie, copyist. He had remittent fever, but lived on until 1912. (Source: Veterans Records, National Archives, Washington, D.C.) After the Civil War, Daniel moved to South Central Missouri, took up farming near Houston Missouri and lived out his life. He was pictured with Nathan and Simon Elliott in a turn of the century picture, but no one is sure where or when the picture was taken.

Daniel was the proprietor of the Elliott Foundry, established in 1875. Its original dimensions were 20 X 40 feet, and was run by horse-power, but became a much larger building, fitted with the best machinery—a twelve horsepower engine. His ironwork was done during the summer and wood-work during the winter season. In the beginning, he owned 20 acres and expanded to 206 acres. He learned his trade from his father, Thomas, working in his father's wagon and general machine shop (Coshocton, OH?) at 12 years of age. By 16, he command a journeyman's wage. In 1853, he engaged in his father's old stand, where he remained until 1862, then enlisted in Co. H, of the Ninety-Seventh Infantry, and served as orderly sergeant until May 15, 1865. After the war, he resumed business at the old stand until the spring of 1867, when he located on a farm in Texas County, Missouri, but soon began work as a carpenter and mechanic. He was a member of the Methodist Episcopal Church, the GAR and a Republican. (From History of Missouri, 1889, complied by Goodspeed including a History of Texas County)

Spouse:	CATHARINE E. HENDERSON
Birth Date:	24 Sep 1835
Death Date:	30 Sep 1903
Death Place:	Pine Lawn Cem., Houston, MO
Spouse Father:	William M. HENDERSON (1806–1884)
Spouse Mother:	Mary Storey?

Spouse Notes: CATHARINE HENDERSON married Daniel in 1855—(ESE 11/17/93)

Marriage Date:	26 Aug 1855
Marriage Place:	COSHOCTION, OHIO

Children:	SANDERS STOREY
	LONZO
	MARY "Lucy"
	WILLIAM T.

(3) 1.14a.3 NEWTON ELLIOTT

Birth Date:	1839
Death Date:	1843
Burial Place:	DIED AS A CHILD

(3) 1.14a.4a NATHAN SAUNDERS ELLIOTT*

Birth Date:	1 Feb 1841
Birth Place:	ROSCOE VILLAGE, OHIO
Christen Place:	LIVED IN OHIO, ILL., IOWA, AND MO.
Death Date:	28 Jun 1915
Death Place:	RUSHVILLE, MO

Burial Place: From their Home to RUSHVILLE CEMETERY

Occupation: UNION SOLDIER, CARPENTER, LUMBER DEALER

Education: PUBLIC SCHOOL IN COSHOCTON, OHIO

Religion: METHODIST

Notes: NATHAN S. ELLIOTT was the third son (Simon, Daniel Gross, Nathan and Thomas) of Thomas (1807–1872?) and Lucy Saunders Elliott (–1842). He was born in Roscoe village, near Coshocton, Ohio. His father was working as a wheelwright. The village is located on the west bank of the Muskingum/Tuscorowas Rivers. Parts of the canal were restored along with the restoration of Roscoe village in the 1970's. He was named for his maternal grandfather, Nathan Saunders. Within 18 months, he and his brothers lost their mother, Lucy. She died around May 20 and was buried, Sunday, May 22, 1842. She was buried in the Methodist Cemetery in Keene near other members of the Elliott family. In 1844, father Thomas married Nancy Nutt (1825?–1870?) and added three children more to his brood. Who assumed the care and raising of the surviving Saunders boys seems to be a family matter that is not clear. Nathan may have learned the carpentry trade from his father. However, he spent a part of his childhood and youth living with his Aunt Jane and her family in Coolville, Ohio. At the time the Civil War broke out, Nathan was living in Coolville, Athens County. He volunteered for the 53rd Regiment of the Ohio Infantry Volunteers, Company B. He joined for three years, at age 20, as a private on October 5, 1861, at Camp Diamond, Ohio, near Jackson, in Athens County. According to his record and military history, October 5 through December 31, 1861, was the basic training period for the regiment, i.e., about 90 days. Nathan was appointed 2nd Corporal on November 2, and issued a Springfield rifled musket along with other members of Co. A and B, while the other company received older musket loaders, i.e. Austrian or French. At the time of his enlistment, and according to his record, he was six feet, one inch tall, had blue eyes, dark hair and by occupation, a carpenter. The only comment on his enlistment record was the name: Miss Mary A. Boyd (single), Coolville, Athens, County, Ohio. The custom was to name someone to notify in case of emergency or death. One could speculate that she was a girlfriend that Nathan met while training at Camp Diamond. More likely, the Boyds were related, and she was a "kissin' cousin."

The 53rd volunteer infantry regiment (OVI) was organized at Camp Diamond, Jackson, Ohio, from October 5, 1861, to February 5, 1862.[7] The original members (except veterans) were mustered out October 3, 1864, by reason of expiration of term of service. The regiment was mustered out of service August 11, 1865, at Little Rock, Arkansas, in accordance with orders from the War Department. The official list of battles included seventeen locations beginning with Shiloh in Tennessee in early April 1862, and ending with the North Edisto River in South Carolina, in February 1865. The regiment was part of the 15th Army Corps (Army of the Tennessee) commanded by U.S. Grant until promoted to higher command, then W.T. Sherman who commanded three Corps, then J. McPherson who was killed at the Battle of Atlanta, and finally O.O. Howard. The 53rd was part of the 5th Division, until the Battle for Atlanta, then assigned to the 2nd Division under M. L. Smith, and 2nd Brigade under J. A. J. Lightburn, later commanded by their former regimental commander, W. S. Jones. During active service, the 53rd was commanded by (1) J. Appler who was forced to resign after Shiloh, then (2) W. S. Jones who was later promoted to Brigade commander, and (3) R. A. Fulton who remained with the Regiment until discharged December 11, 1864. The regiment marched through Tennessee, Mississippi, Alabama, Georgia and both Carolinas.

In 1862, near the beginning of the western conflict in the Tennessee area, Grant was appointed commander of the Army of Western Tennessee, with Sherman and others under his command. In the fall of 1963, shortly after the Battle of Chickamauga and before the Battle of Chattanooga, Lincoln decided to consolidate the western command with Grant in charge of all Union troops. The command was composed of three armies. The largest was the Army of the Cumberland under Thomas, while the Army of the Ohio under Schofield the smallest, and the Army of the Tennessee was the third unit. Nathan traveled in eight states with the Army of Tennessee, roughly composed of seventy-one regiments, or 30,000 officers and men. Their commanding officer was (1) Wm. T. Sherman, until promoted, followed by (2) James B. McPherson until he was killed at Atlanta, and then by (3) W.S. Jones.

At the end of the conflict, the 53rd OVI was part of the Second Division, Fifteenth Army Corp. The Regiment traveled 6400 miles, engaged in sixty-seven battles and skirmishes, lost sixty officers and men killed, and two hundred and sixty-four officers and men wounded. Unfortunately, the 53rd was badly embarrassed at Shiloh, when they were overrun by attacking Confederate units.[28] On the positive side, their major successful campaigns included the Campaign for Vicksburg (Sherman faced defeat at Chickasaw Bluff while the 53rd was chasing

Van Dorn near Holly Springs, Miss., and were later transported to Haines Bluff where they joined a march to the Big Black River to frustrate Johnson's effort to relieve Vicksburg) and the battle over Missionary Ridge, near Chattanooga, Tenn. Other major campaigns included the march through Georgia during the Atlanta Campaign and the march to the sea and capture of Savannah in 1864. The winter campaign of '65 through South and North Carolina finally ended in the victory parade through Washington D.C.[29]

Nathan rose through the enlisted ranks during his enlistment. He made 3rd Sergeant, November 1, 1862, and re-enlisted at age 22 in Scottsboro, Alabama, June 1, 1864. At that time, the 53rd was closing their winter camp and preparing for the assault on Atlanta. Enlistment of veterans was a growing concern for the Federals. In late May, Sherman was trying to outflank Joe Johnston's Confederate units during the battle for Dallas, Georgia. For the next 100 days, the armies were on the move in constant contact with the enemy, and never had opportunity to sleep easy, prepare meals, or take a bath. For the most part, the three armies shifted from end to end in order to outflank Johnston's defenses. At Kennesaw Mountain, the 53rd was part of a direct assault with hand-to-hand combat on Little Kennesaw Mountain that failed to break the rebel line. In September 1864, Nathan was promoted to 1st Sergeant after the capture of Atlanta.

On May 20, 1865, as the war ended, he was commissioned a 1st Lieutenant and stayed with Co. B until discharged on the 11th day of August 1865 in Little Rock Arkansas. [50] In January, February and March of '63, Nathan's outfit had a month furlough. They boarded a northbound train on the evening of January 25th, 1864, headed for Nashville, homeward bound on a veteran's furlough. They reached Nashville on the 27th, then traveled to Cincinnati, Ohio where they reformed on March 12 in order to return to Scottsboro, Ala., their winter quarters. Nathan probably stayed in Nashville, Tennessee to visit his brother (Thomas) who was recovering from wounds received at Chickamauga.

Following his discharge from the army of occupation in Arkansas (August, 1865), Nathan journeyed north to visit his father in Ohio or more likely Illinois. Meanwhile, his younger brother Thomas met and married his Illinois wife while recovering from his war wounds in Nashville. Nathan came to visit them in Illinois and stayed in Sangamon County to marry Martha Mallicent Yates (1845–1881) on March 28, 1867, near Berlin, Illinois. Martha gave birth to two children, Ira Elliott, born December 12, 1869, and Lillie C. Elliott, born June 20, 1871. The family lived in Illinois for about six years, 1865–1871, then moved west to Iowa briefly, and on to Craig, Missouri in 1877. Nathan took up the carpentry business. He built their home at 203 Main St. where Martha died early in the winter of 1881. She was probably buried in a local cemetery, near Craig, but we have no record.

In June 1884, Nathan, who was now 43 years of age, climbed down into the well on their property to clean it out. When he came out of the well, the cold water had chilled his legs, and they gave way. He was unable to work for three months, and his legs gave him trouble for the rest of his life. During this time, he met and married his second wife, Ardilla Lee Redmon (12 Jul. 1863–22 Feb. 1916). They married December 20, 1885. William Redmon, her father, lived in Holt County, and probably farmed near Craig. "Ardie Lee" was a life-long resident of Craig and had known Nathan for some time. Their five children, born in Craig, were Earl Saunders (3 Dec 1887–14 Jul. 1944), Benjamin Franklin (14 Jan 1891–28 Aug. 1944), Charles Metz (6 Jun 1896–24 Jun 1951), Grace Maxine (31 Oct. 1898–16 Jul. 1961) and Ruth Isabella (1 Apr. 1901–28 Aug. 1975.

The family lived in Craig until 1904. During his later years, Nathan tried lumber dealing as a way to make a living, and traveled to the Ozarks where the boys helped haul lumber on Elliott Hill. They lived out their lives in northwest Missouri, except for two years when they moved to Winona (1905–07), a southern Missouri town in Shannon County, to practice the lumber trade. He applied for a veteran's pension in March 16, 1907, (age 65). The medical board reviewed his case and indicated that he had varicose veins in both legs. In due time his petition was approved. After Ardilla Lee broke her leg early in 1908, they returned to Rushville, near St. Joseph. With declining health, Nathan lived to age 74, and died June 28, 1915. Ardilla applied for widow and child benefits, since Ruth, the youngest child, was under 16 years of age. Ardilla Lee lived on for only six months.

Earl became Ruth's guardian, when their mother, Ardilla Lee, died, February 22, 1916. In the application papers, Eva Redmon Burke and her husband signed as witnesses. Eva was a sister of Ardilla Lee who lived in St. Joseph at the time. The marriage license for Nathan and Ardilla Lee (Arda) was filed in the County Court House in Oregon, Missouri, Holt County. Elizabeth Elliott gave (18 Nov. 1962) a set of veteran papers of Nathan S. Elliot to Grace Miller so that application for a military grave head stone could be documented.[36]

Spouse:	MARTHA MALICENT YATES
Birth Date:	11 Jun 1845
Birth Place:	NEAR BERLIN IL, ISLAND GROVE, SANGOMON
Death Date:	20 Dec 1881
Death Place:	CRAIG, MO. of Winter Fever
Burial Place:	CRAIG, MO? no record of cemetery
Occupation:	HOMEMAKER & MOTHER OF TWO
Education:	ISLAND GROVE COUNTRY SCHOOL
Religion:	METHODIST
Spouse Father:	THOMAS YATES (1811–1870)
Spouse Mother:	NANCY HIGGINS (1816–1860)

MARTHA M. YATES. After Nathan was dischared from the service, he returned north to visit his father in Ohio or more likely Illinois. He stayed in Sagamon county to marry Martha Malicent Yates (1845–1881) on March 28, 1867, near Berlin, Illinois. They had two children, Iry Elliott, born December 12, 1869, and Cora "Lillie" Lillian Elliott, born June 20, 1871. The family lived in Illinois for about six years, 1865–1871, then moved west to Iowa briefly, and on to Craig, Missouri. They arrived in Craig, 1 August 1877. Martha died during the winter of 1881. She was one of 10 living children. Her father, Thomas (14 Mar, 1811) was born in Gallatin county, Kentucky, was married 29 Mar 1837, at Berlin, Ill to Nancy Higgins, (23 May 1816) who came with her parents to Sangamon county in 1836 (She died 15 Dec, 1860). (Living Descendants of Early Settlers of Sagamon County) The family was related to Richard Yates who was elected Governor of Illinois in 1856 (Civil War), and her Great Uncle was John Marshall (U.S. Supreme Court Judge). They lived in Island Groove Township outside of Springfield. Thomas farmed 600 acres.

Marriage Date:	22 Mar 1867
Marriage Place:	recorded as 03/28/1867 in BERLIN, SANGAMON CO., ILL.
Children:	IRA YATES
	CORA "LILLIE" LILLIAN

Other spouses: ARDELL(I)A LEE REDMON

*(3) 1.14a.4b NATHAN SAUNDERS ELLIOTT**

(See above)

Spouse:	ARDELL(I)A LEE REDMON
Birth Date:	12 Jul 1863
Birth Place:	CRAIG, HOLT COUNTY, MO
Death Date:	22 Feb 1916
Death Place:	RUSHVILLE, MO
Burial Place:	Armstrong CEMETERY, RUSHVILLE, MO
Occupation:	HOUSEWIFE & MOTHER OF FIVE
Education:	CRAIG PUBLIC SCHOOLS
Spouse Father:	WILLIAM T. REDMON (1824–1906)
Spouse Mother:	SARAH ISGRIGG (1839–1887)

Spouse Notes: ARDELL(I)A LEE REDMON ELLIOTT. Nathan met Arda while he was recovering from his bout with the well. They married December 20, 1885. William Redmon, her father, lived in Holt County, and probably farmed near Craig. "Ardie Lee" was a life-long resident of Craig and had known Nathan for some time. Their five children, all born in Craig, were Earl Saunders (12/3/1887–7/14/44), Benjamin Franklin (1/14/1891–8/28/1944), Charles Metz (6/6/1896–6/24/51), Grace (8/31/1898–7/16/1961) and Ruth I. (4/2/1901–8/24/1975). The family lived in Craig until 1904. During his later years, Nathan had taken up lumber dealing as a way to make a living, and traveled to the Ozarks where the boys helped haul lumber. They bought a section of land near Winona in Shannon County, Mo. The price was 50 cents an acre when they bought and 25 cents when they sold the same land a year later. In 1904, Earl was 16 and Ben 14. Ardilla fell and broke her leg, so they returned to Rushville, Mo.

Ira Elliott had a place built for them to live on the edge of town, near a large tree, along the cement road to St. Joe. The tree still stands (1992), but the house was washed away by floods during the 1930's. He first applied for a veteran pension March 11, 1901 (Age 60), and again, March 16, 1907, (age 65) when they moved from Craig to a southern Missouri town called Winona, in Shannon

County. The medical board reviewed his case and indicated that he had varicose veins in both legs. In due time his petition was approved. By early 1908, they returned to Rushville, near St. Joseph, after Ardilla broke her leg. She never really recovered from the injury.

Ardella Lee "Arda" wrote to her son, "Charley" when he was in "Telegraphic" school in Chillicothe, Mo., Livingston County.[37] He started to school there in the early spring of 1913.[8] In the letter (Sep. 14, 1914), she wrote about family matters, the weather, old "Red" the milk cow, and connections for coming home to visit. Nathan died at age 74, June 28, 1915.

Ardella Lee lived on for only six months after Nathan died. She applied for widow and child benefits, since Ruth, the youngest child, was under 16 years of age. Earl became Ruth's guardian, when their mother, Ardella Lee, died, February 22, 1916. She died of bleeding from female complications. In the application papers, Eva Redmon Burke and her husband signed as witnesses. Eva was the only sister of Ardella Lee (although they had several half brothers and sisters) who lived in St. Joseph at the time. The marriage license for Nathan S. Elliot(t) and Arda Redmon (Ardella Lee Redmon) was filed (20 Dec 1885) in the County Court House in Oregon, Missouri, Holt County.

Marriage Date:	20 Dec 1885
Marriage Place:	CRAIG, MO (Witness Elder Blaine)
Children:	EARL SAUNDERS
	BENJAMIN FRANKLIN
	CHARLES METZ
	GRACE MAXINE
	RUTH ISABELLA
Other spouses:	MARTHA MALICENT YATES

(3) 1.14a.5 THOMAS ELLIOTT

Birth Date:	25 Mar 1842
Birth Place:	COSHOCTON COUNTY, OHIO

Death Date:	14 Mar 1899
Death Place:	DAWSON, ILL.
Burial Place:	DAWSON, ILL.
Occupation:	SERVED IN UNION ARMY (51TH OVI)
Education:	LEFT HOME AT AGE 16
Religion:	METHODIST

Notes: THOMAS ELLIOTT was the youngest of five brothers. He was born in 1842, as his mother lay weakened by a flu-like infection. She died about six weeks after he was born. He was cared for by family members until he reached the age of majority (age 16) when he went to work on his own. He joined the 51st OVI at Spring Mountain as a private when he was 18 years old. The regiment was composed mostly of Coshocton County boys. The history of the 51st OVI was included in the History of Coshocton County, Ohio, published by A.A. GRAHM & CO., Newark Ohio, 1881, pp, 337–344. Thomas was listed as a private in Company I. The 51st OVI was composed of many boys from Coshocton County. Thomas joined the 51st OVI, Company I, for three years at Spring Mountain, Ohio, Sept 18, 1861, as a private, by J.M. Crooks.

When he volunteered for the OVI, he was 19 years old, 5ft., 7 in. in height, had light complexion, eyes were blue, and hair dark. He was detached as a Division teamster, Camp Wickliffer, Kentucky, Jan 7, 1862, by order of Gen. Nelson. In May-Aug, he was temporarily detached for service in artillery. Later, he was wounded in action at the Battle of Munfreesboro (Dec. 30–Jan 3) on Stones River, Tenn. Jan 2, 1863. (source: Report of Gen. Rosencrans, pp. 498) He was wounded in the left thigh and a patient in the Hospital at Covington, Ky and Camp Dennison, Ohio. He rejoined his outfit for duty May 25, 1863. On Sept 19, 1863, he was missing in action at Chickamauga, and later reported wounded in the right side on the casulty sheet. He was on the Hospital Muster Roll at Nashville, Tenn. and Covington, Ky., through a large part of his remaining enlistment. He was mustered out near Vilanow, Georgia., Oct. 17, 1864, when his clothing account was settled with a money adv'd of $78.41. He received $100 due, subsistence and transportation to Nashville, Tennessee when he was dischared by reason of expiration of terms of service. (source: Veterans Records, National Archives, Washington, D.C.)[39]

Unit location during Battle of Chickamauga (19 SEP 1863), 14TH CORPS—THOMAS:, 3RD DIV—VAN CLEVE:, 3RD BRIGADE—BARNES: 51TH OVI—McCLAIN/WOOD located at marker #248 near Barnes Bridge

He moved to Berlin, Illinois after the war, raised a family in Dawson, Illinois and died there in 1899. In 1975, Earl Elliott, Jr. found a voter registration record (dated Oct. 17, 1865) in the Clayville coach stop, about 2 miles east from Pleasant Plains, and west of Springfield, Illinois, while visiting the restored building. The register listed Thomas Elliott, as living in Berlin, 10 miles west of Springfield, off the old Jacksonville Road. At that time, he lived in Cartwright Township (formerly Island Groove?), Sangamon County. He married Sarah Dawson (1865?) and moved to Dawson, Illinois where he farmed until his death in 1899.

Spouse:	Sarah Adaline DAWSON
Birth Date:	1845
Birth Place:	DAWSON, IL
Death Date:	1899
Occupation:	HOUSEWIFE
Religion:	METHODIST
Spouse Father:	James H. Dawson (1821–1911)
Spouse Mother:	Elizabeth McLaughlin (1827–1890)

Spouse Notes: Sarah Dawson probably met Thomas while he was in the hospital in Covington, Kentucky or Nashville, Tennessee. She was a volunteer who went south to help through a Methodist Church group. Her family settled the town of Dawson, Illinois.

Marriage Date:	26 Jun 1865
Marriage Place:	DAWSON, SANGAMON CO., Ill.
Children:	Minnie Elizabeth
	Etta B.
	William Arthur

*(2) 1.14b THOMAS ELLIOTT**

(See above)

Spouse:	NANCY NUTT
Birth Date:	13 Jun 1816
Birth Place:	Topsham, Orange, VT, near Montpelier
Death Date:	About 1903
Death Place:	Mackinaw, IL
Occupation:	STEPMOTHER OF 3 & MOTHER OF 4
Education:	tracing back to Mayflower?

Spouse Notes: NANCY NUTT Nancy married Thomas in Coshocton in 1844. Their marriage is recorded in the public records in the Coshocton Court House. The marriage produced four children: Charles H., David S., Napoleon B and Lucy. Her relationship with her stepchildren was reported as stormy. A letter from Nathan to George (his Uncle) indicated that she felt Thomas was partial to the Saunders rather than the Nutt children. Son, Thomas left home at age 16 (1856) and joined the 51th OVI (1861). The Biographical data on C.H. Elliott says that Nancy Nutt was born near Montpelier, Vermont, and is descended from old Puritan stock, her ancestors having probably come to this country on the Mayflower. (Nancy Harvey, 8/12/98)

Marriage Date:	26 Sep 1844
Marriage Place:	COSHOCTON, OHIO
Children:	CHARLES H.
	David S.
	Napoleon B.
	Lucy
Other spouses:	LUCY W. SAUNDERS

(3) 1.14b.1 CHARLES H. ELLIOTT

Birth Date:	6 Aug 1845
Birth Place:	COSHOCTON, OHIO
Death Date:	25 Jun 1930
Death Place:	age 84
Burial Place:	Union Cemetery, WINFIELD, KANS.
Occupation:	Machinist, Rancher in Cowley Co., KS since 1884
Education:	Ohio, Illinois (age 9 +) Sangamon Co

Notes: Charles had two sons, Samuel & Charles (another Charley). They lived in Winfield, Kansas. He had the Family Bible, according to E.C. Elliott (1955). Charles H. Elliott owned 1,194 acres, and operated over 3000 acres near Winfield, KS at the turn of the 19th Century....In the Spring of 1854, when nine years of age, Charles went to Sangamon County, Illinois, and after residing there many years located in Kansas, spending the first two years in Neosha County, where he improved a farm. He then went to Greenwood, where he spent four years, and on Oct. 23, 1884, he settled on the northwest quarter of section 16, township 31, range 5, east, where he made his home. Each year, he cultivated crops (corn and alfalfa) and handled over 1000 head of Shorthorn cattle, as well as 15,000 or more Portland-China hogs. (Source:[21] Biographical Sketches, Leading Citizens of Cowley Co., 1901. From the Winfield Public Library, Winfield, KS)

Spouse:	MARGARET THOMPKINS
Birth Date:	1846
Birth Place:	Belleville, Canada
Death Place:	about age 65 of Tuberculosis
Burial Place:	Union Cemetery, WINFIELD, KANS.
Occupation:	Children: Anna Maud, Emma Ethel, Samuel, Charles"Mike"
Education:	Spoke French
Religion:	Episcopalian

Spouse Father:	John THOMPKINS
Spouse Mother:	Margaret Clutes

Spouse Notes: Charles married Margaret Tompkins in Missouri. She was born in 1846, at Belleville, Canada, who is a daughter of John and Margaret (Clutes) Tompkins, both her parents are Canadians. There were 12 children in the Tompkins family, seven of whom reached their majority.

Marriage Date:	1871
Marriage Place:	Illinois or Missouri
Children:	Anna Maud
	Emma Ethel
	Samuel
	CHARLES THOMPKINS "Mike"

(3) 1.14b.2 David S. ELLIOTT

Birth Date:	23 May 1847
Birth Place:	COSHOCTON, OHIO
Death Date:	12 Nov 1912
Burial Place:	BELLVILLE, ILL.
Spouse:	Emily MULBERGER

(3) 1.14b.3 Napoleon B. ELLIOTT

Birth Date:	8 Apr 1849
Birth Place:	COSHOCTON, OHIO
Death Date:	6 Mar 1852
Burial Place:	COSHOCTON, OHIO
Education:	died as an infant of a complaint

Notes: Father, Thomas still had the "itch" to go to California, buy some land, and return to Coshocton. He thought that his wife & children could handle his absence. His brothers, George and Samuel paid Thomas a brotherly visit and talked him out of going west.

(3) 1.14b.4 Lucy ELLIOTT

Birth Date:	25 Jul 1856
Birth Place:	COSHOCTON, OHIO
Death Date:	17 Aug 1933
Burial Place:	CEDAR COUNTY, IOWA
Occupation:	1901–living with her mother in Mackinaw, IL

Lucy never married. She was musical. For a part of her life, she lived with her aging mother, Nancy Nutt Elliott, in Mackinaw, Illinois, about 20 miles south of Peorio. Her mother, Nancy, lived until about 1905. Then Lucy moved to Cedar County, Iowa where she died in 1931.

(2) 1.15 SIMON ELLIOTT

Birth Date:	25 Oct 1809
Birth Place:	DONEGAL, IRELAND
Christen Date:	1827
Christen Place:	converted and joined the M.E. Church
Death Date:	24 Sep 1849
Death Place:	Fulton County, ILL
Burial Place:	WELLSVILLE, COLUMBIANA CO., OHIO
Occupation:	METHODIST MINISTER, presiding elder
Education:	MADISON COLLEGE, UNIONTOWN, PA
Religion:	SUPERVISED BY BROTHER, CHARLES ELLIOTT

Notes: SIMON ELLIOTT Presiding Elder of Steubenville District in the Pittsburgh Conference at the time of his death. He was educated at Madison College,

Uniontown, PA under the supervision of his brother, Charles Elliott who was Professor of Literature at Madison College (1827–1831). He joined the Pittsburgh Conference in 1833 and held a number of leading positions in the Methodist Conference.

Simon Elliott's Will recorded Uttica, March 1, 1845, County of Fulton, State of Illinois appointed John Elliott, son of John Elliott, and Andrew Elliott, son of William Elliott to be executors wanted "all my property equally divided between my brothers' children"

Rev. Simon Elliott is buried in the middle of a circle of Elliotts in the New Springfield Cemetery on top a bluff overlooking Wellsville, OH.

Spouse Notes: CHRISTIANI GROFF ELLIOTT In a letter from Mary Ann Boyd to her parents in Coolville (1849), she reported that her Uncle Simon had been in Keene and told her that his wife was not feeling well at all.

Spouse:	CHRISTIANI GROFF
Birth Date:	1810
Birth Place:	WELLSVILLE, OHIO
Marriage Date:	8 Jun 1841
Marriage Place:	WELLSVILLE, OHIO

Researching Elliott Family History/Stories

1. Frances Blaine Elliott (1764–1845) by Blanche Elliott, 1941.

2. Settlement Lands in Mill Creek and Keene Townships, Coshocton and Holmes Counties, State of Ohio and Burial Headstones in Keene M.E. Cemetery by John Frizell "Lell" Elliott, Jr.

3. A History of the Keene Churches by Jay Lawrence, 1968.

4. Story of Isabella Blaine and George Elliott

5. 100 Years in America 1820–1920 by Daniel D. and Augusta Crawford Boyd.

6. (M1) James Elliott, (N2) Samuel Elliott, (F–1) Mary Ann (A) Daniel Boyd.

7. Elgin P. Kintner/Mildred King Johasson traced family to Mary Elliott.

8. History of Coshocton Co. Ohio by W. E. Hunt, 1876.

9. James Elliott, oldest son of John and Fanny Blaine Elliott lived in Holmes Co.

10. Moses Elliott Family from Pennsylvania to Ohio to Missouri

11. Andrew Elliott lived in Ireland, Coshocton and Iowa

12. Charles Elliott, Methodist Minister in Pennsylvania, Ohio, Missouri, and Iowa.

13. John Elliott, Rebel Son, Presbyterian and Builder of Local Churches

14. Samuel Elliott lived most of his life in Coshocton County

15. Anne Elliott Shaffer lived a Short Life

16. Jane Elliott Boyd & Her Irish Sweetheart Lived in Coshocton and Athens Co.

17. Simon Elliott lived in Coshocton Ohio, Uniontown, Penns and Wellsville, Ohio

18. Thomas Elliott lived in Holmes Co., Coshocton, Ohio, Dawson, Illinois, and Guilford, Kansas.

19. Thomas Elliott and second wife, Nancy Nutt

20. Simon Elliott, oldest son of Thomas Elliott

21. Daniel Gross Elliott—second son of Thomas Elliott lived in Ohio and Missouri.

22. Nathan Saunders, third son of T. Elliott lived in Ohio, Illinois and Missouri.

23. Martha Mallicent Yates, first wife of Nathan S. Elliott, lived in Illinois and Missouri.

24. Families of Ira Yates Elliott & Children, Cecil, Willis and Ira Jr.

25. Manasa P. Lay—Missouri Brigade, Confederate States, lived in Missouri.

26. Families of Cora Lillian "Lilly" Elliott Inman

27. Elliott, Thomas—son of Thomas Elliott lived in Ohio and Illinois.

28. Record of the Family as given by Mary Finlay Hester, Jan. 30, 1903

29. Genealogy of the David and Alice Finlay Family

30. Finlay Family in Ohio

31. Saunders Family from England to Rhode Island to California

32. Isgrigg Family from England to Kentucky, Illinois and Missouri

33. Carlton Family from England to New England and West

34. Redmon(d) Family line from Kentucky to Illinois to Missouri.

35. Madison Redmon, oldest child of George and Eda

36. William T. Redmon Family Line in Kentucky, Illinois and Missouri

Sources of Elliott Family Information & Stories

Online Elliott Family Sources:

Our Blaine/Boyd/Elliott/Finlay/Saunders/Redmon/Isgrigg family history in the New World includes over 3,500 names in the genealogy with stories about many family members. Check out the following online sources:

http://homepages.rootsweb.com/~eelliott/WC_TOC.HTM#CNTC
Online genealogy of Nathan Saunders Elliott family lines. The file includes sets of family pictures and stories.

http://www.myfamily.com/isapi.
dll?c=content&htx=list&siteid=*&contentclass=PICT
Collection of Elliott family pictures, reports, news and other information. Check with exe1@psu.edu for gaining access codes.

Brief descriptions of many sources, some interesting stories and a list of references are included. For example, Earl e-mailed a reply to an inquiry) which began in the spring of 1998. Earl posted a message on the Missouri Pioneers web page of the Roots program seeking information about Jesse Isgrigg. At the '98 Reunion, Janet Elliott Ewart shared her data on the female genealogy of the Elliott family, i.e. Redmon, Saunders, Isgrigg, Carlton. On the following Monday, a small group of cousins visited the Canton Private Cemetery near Mound City, MO and located the graves of Jesse T. Isgrigg, his wife Jane Johnson Isgrigg, and their daughter, Sarah Isgrigg Redmon. During the next six months, Earl used e-mail contacts to locate sources collected by other people interested in locating and sharing family names, dates and other information regarding these surnames. Each search was completed with success, for **Saunders, Redmon, Carlton and Isgrigg family lines**. The female side of the family seemed more complicated to research, probably due to factors such as name changes in a male-dominated society and the hidden value of women. The information was available, but overlooked.

Great grandfather Thomas Elliott married Lucy Saunders, grandfather Nathan Saunders Elliott was named for his mother's father, Nathan **Saunders**. Our grandmother, Ardella **Redmon** was a daughter of William T. Redmon and Sarah Isgrigg, William T. was a son of George W. and Eda **Carlton**, while Eda was a daughter of Kimball Carlton and Elizabeth Spillman, and Sarah was a daughter of Jesse H. **Isgrigg** and Jane Johnson. Still, the Redmon connection offers the most confusing data; i.e. "George" Redmon was a common name in Hardin County, Kentucky, at the beginning of the 19th Century. Several BLAINE sisters arrived in Ohio with their Irish families as states like Ohio organized the Northwest. The oldest sister was Isabella (1750–?), then Alice (1760–?), Frances (1764–1845) and possibly another unknown sister (1760–?). Each married Elliott, Boyd, or Finlay men in Ireland. They came to America and brought their children as the new nation emerged around the turn of the 18th century. Protestant families kept family Bibles and recorded their own birth, marriage and death information. Records of Irish protestant families, especially Methodists, were poorly recorded. The official recorder of vital statistics was the Church of England or the Roman Catholic churches. Methodists were considered a radical and rebellious group of people. These Methodists often refused to provide the official church with useful information. Records were used for tax collection, property identification (wives and children), and military recruitment. The government encouraged them to leave Ireland by providing shipping tickets for widows with large families of young children, and facilitated land sales in the Colonies.

The older daughter, Isabella Blaine, married the original George Elliott in Ireland. There was war in Europe and conscription of Irish young men for the British army and navy was a common event. To escape, families turned to the land across the ocean. The American Colonies offered political and religious freedom as well as land with opportunity to grow. Apparently, Isabella settled in the new lands in Pennsylvania or Northwest Territory, but no one is certain where she and her family lived. One of Isabella's sons, Aaron, served in the War of 1812 with a Virginia company (West Virginia). Eventually, Aaron lived in Rose Twp. of Carroll Co., near Coshocton Co., Ohio where "Bell's" younger sister, Frances "Fanny" and her family lived.

"Fanny" Blaine Elliott brought several (some say eight) (James, Moses, Andrew, Charles, John, George, Samuel, Anne, Jane, Thomas, and Simon) of her children from Donegal, Ireland to Ohio in 1816. Fanny held 200 acres and son George held 100 acres in the same township on Doughty Creek. This land was then located in Coshocton County and would be until 1824 when a new county was formed in the north, Holmes County. While living here, Fanny's daughter Jane married Daniel Boyd in 1825, who was living with his father, Robert, east of Keene. Fanny's son, Andrew (1790–1863) stayed near Doughty Creek when Fanny moved a few miles south with her son George (1798–1875) into what became Mill Creek Township of Coshocton County, Ohio. Thus began confusion about Elliott cousins and who lived where and how they were related.

Family Information and Brief Comments

1. Frances Blaine Elliott (1764–1845) by Blanche Elliott, 1941.

In the summer of 1941, Blanche Elliott (1890–1960), 1136 Orchard Street, Coshocton, Ohio, entered the Ohioana Library Essay Contest. She received Honorable Mention placing 6th in a field of 90 essays. Her essay began with a poem she wrote about Frances Blaine Elliott (1764–1845) and continued with 17 pages of family information. The manuscript on Fanny Blaine Elliott was the first and most important document on Elliott/Blaine Family History. It was widely copied and shared in different parts of the family. Janet Elliott Ewart gave a copy to Elizabeth C. Elliott in the late 1950's. The document was an important stimulus to family study because so little was included about Thomas Elliott.

Elliott, Blanche, "Frances Blaine Elliott," unpublished manuscript, honorable mention in Ohioana Library Essay Contest, Coshocton, Ohio, 1941. Copies of Unpublished Documents are available in the Genealogy Section of the Coshocton Public Library, Coshocton, Ohio.

2. Settlement Lands in Mill Creek and Keene Townships, Coshocton and Holmes Counties, State of Ohio and Burial Headstones in Keene M.E. Cemetery by John Frizell "Lell", Jr.

James Elliott (1782–1849), oldest son of John & Fanny Blaine Elliott came to America in 1819. He and his family settled in what became Mechanic Township, Holmes County, Ohio. His g-g-g-grandson, "Lell" collected family history, visited Holmes County and Coshocton County several times during summer academic breaks. He documented the location of graves in the Elliott Cemetery in Mechanic Township, Holmes Co., the Elliott Chapel on the grounds of Samuel Elliott home and the Lower Methodist Cemetery in Keene, OH. Before he died,

John F. "Lell" Elliott, Jr. (1908–1993) gave copies of his work to his cousin, Melvin Elliott.

Elliott, John Frizell "Lell" Elliott Jr., great-grandson of James collected family history of James Elliott line of descendants. He visited Coshocton County several times during the 1970's, made maps of the Elliott Cemetery and Keene U.M. Cemetery and documented the James' generational line.

3. A History of the Keene Churches by Jay Lawrence, 1968.

The story of Presbyterian and Methodist Churches in Keene, Ohio. Elliott, Boyd and information were gathered from descendants of George Elliott (1798–1875). Blanche Elliott, Zelma Wheatcraft and daughter Alicia Oldham, Laura Croft and Emma Norton were active family historians. They tried to understand the marriage between George and Mary Elliott.

Lawrence, Jay, A History of the Keene Churches, 1968, pp. 1–15. Based on family records of Zelma Wheatcraft regarding the Elliott family and their settlement in Coshocton County in 1816 and participation in the establishment of the U.M. Church in Keene.

4. Story of Isabella Blaine and George Elliott

Several Blaine sisters and their families came to America between 1790 & 1820. The oldest sister was probably Isabella (1750–?), then Alice (1760–?), and Frances (1764–1845). Each married Elliott, Boyd or Finlay men in Ireland. All of them came to America and brought their children to the Northwest as the new nation emerged at the turn of the 18th century.

George & Isabella Blaine Elliott lived in Southwest Pennsylvania and their son, Andrew W., lived in Eastern Ohio, around Stubenville and later moved west to Holmes County, Ohio. Fannie Blaine Elliott's own son, Andrew (1790–1863) stayed in the Holmes County area when Francis (Fannie) moved south, just across the county line to Coshocton County, to live with her son George (1798–1875) in the Mill Creek Township area of Coshocton County.

After the death of George Elliott about 1799, Isabelle with ten children left Northern Ireland for America. They settled in Washington Co., Pennsylvania.

"Blacksmith" George was born in Ireland and came to America in about 1802 with his parents and grandparents who probably settled along the Ohio River. The Eastern edge of Ohio along the Ohio River, became Stubenville, Ohio. The family lived in Smithfield Township, Jefferson County, Ohio when son, Hugh W. was born (1821). Five years later, when their second child, Jane, was born (1826), the family lived in Mechanic Township, Holmes County, Ohio.

To distinguish this George Elliott (1792–1868) from another George Elliott (1798–1875) living in the same area, he acquired the nickname "Blacksmith" where he operated a farm and blacksmith shop in Holmes County. Later, he deeded two acres of his land (1846) for the Elliott Church in Mechanic Township, Holmes County, about three miles from Clark, Ohio on Route #85.

The land on which the Elliotts settled in Coshocton County, Ohio lay mostly on the divide between Tom's Run and Military Creek. These lots were almost contiguous extended in a northern direction from Lot 25 in the south:

a.   From Lot 25 settled by James Elliott in 1819 to the lots of Andrew Elliott's 140–acre farm was a distance of almost two miles.

b.   George Elliott Sr. (Blacksmith George) settled on Lot 24 in 1819. After living there for 35 years, he transferred ownership to his eldest son Robert who lived there until his death in 1900. At the time of the transfer George bought the west half of Lot 18 and lived there until his death in 1868.

c.   Samuel Elliott, a son of George and brother of Robert settled on Lot 19 that Andrew Elliott first bought. He settled there and later bought Lot 20.

d.   Andrew's oldest son when married purchased the Lot laying directly west of Andrews.

e.   Andrew's [2nd] son, James C. bought Lot "1 laying just west of Lot 19 and lived thereon until his death in 1880. He seemed to have been a very progressive farmer having two fair sized orchards with various kinds of delicious fruit. He also had a large two-story frame house, a frame outhouse into which he had running water piped from a spring some distance north east of the house. About three years after his death, A.W. Logsdon purchased the farm. (Source: description by A.W. Logsdon's son, Harry C. Logsdon, author of Silent Streams.)

Heiser, Hugh Arlan. Unpublished Collection of Elliott Family Information, Letters beginning in 1965 through 1996.

5. One Hundred Years in America 1820–1920 by Daniel D and Augusta Crawford Boyd.

Boyd, Elliott and Finlay families intermarried in Ireland and continued to do so in Ohio. The Albert Boyd family was located in Donegal, Ireland like the Elliotts and Finales. and came to America in the early years to settle in Pennsylvania and Ohio. The families were tied together by several Blaine sisters who married Boyd, Elliott and Finlay men in Ireland and brought their families to the New World to escape Ireland for religious and political reasons as well as greater economic opportunity.

Boyd, Daniel D. & Augusta Crawford Boyd, One Hundred Years in America 1820–1920. Genealogy of the Family of Albert Boyd, Ireland.. Unpublished booklet, 1920.

6. (M1) James Elliott, (N2) Samuel Elliott, (F–1) Mary Ann Boyd (A) Daniel Boyd.

Several letters written in the 1840's through 1860's communicated the words of these cousins about the death of Lucy Saunders, life in Keene, OH and attitudes about the Civil War:

(M1) James Elliott wrote (11 Apr 1842) to his sister and her family in Coolville, Ohio following the death of Lucy Saunders Elliott,
(N2) Samuel Elliott (Jun 16, 1842) wrote after the funeral of Lucy,
(F–1) Mary Ann (Mar 23, 1849) wrote to her parents from Keene, Ohio, and Uncle Daniel to his nephew Nathan near the end of the Civil War (Mar 28, 1865).

The actual letters were saved by Jane Elliott Boyd and discovered in a small box years later. They were difficult to read since the ink was badly faded, the spelling was contemporary and the context was unknown. Yet, volunteers at Roscoe Village Foundation successfully translated the letters and made them available to interested parties.

Norton, Ruth M., great-granddaughter of George Elliott and historian at Roscoe Village, wrote in a letter to Earl S. Elliott Jr., reported finding a letter (June 16th 1842) written by Samuel Elliott to his brother-in-law, Daniel Boyd (Athens County). James Elliott to his brother-in-law, Daniel Boyd (Athens County). Maryann Boyd to her mother and father, Jane Elliott Boyd & Daniel Boyd (Athens County), Daniel Boyd (Athens County) to Nathan Elliott (53rd OVI) about the politics of the War, written near the end of the Civil War, 1865. Roscoe Village Foundation.

7. Elgin P. Kintner/Mildred King Johasson traced family to Mary (Marie) Elliott.

A family history of Edward Kintner (1879–1975) and Glada Snyder (1884–1972) provides an ancestral genealogy and tour guide of several regions where his family lived. Mary (1786–1816), daughter of John and Fanny Blaine Elliott, married James McKee, Jun 6, 1803, in Donegal, Ireland. Their daughter, Isabella McKee came to America, married William Walker, became a widow with two children and lived in Defiance Co., Ohio. The writer, Elgin P. Kintner was one of their g-g-g-g-g-grandchildren. Likewise, Mildred King Johasson (1909–1994) and Esther Janene Critcher were cousins tracing family connections together with Elgin Kintner. The name "George" and Coshocton/Holmes Elliott families remained a challenge. It took years to successfully distinguish between various related Elliott families living in Holmes and Coshocton Counties.

Kintner, E. P., Edward Kintner and Glada Snyder Ancestral Genealogy and Tour Guide, 1994. Published: 1314 Turnberry Lane., Maryville, Tennessee 37801. The Personal family history follows eight generations that includes Mary Elliott.

8. History of Coshocton Co. Ohio by W. E. Hunt, 1876.

The book is a comprehensive history of Ohio, Coshocton County, Townships, Towns, Villages, Schools and Churches. It contains several interesting portraits of early settlers and its soldiers in the late Civil War. See pages 340, Thomas Elliott; pp. 362, Daniel Gross Elliott; pp. 476–77, Doughty Creek; pp. 525, Keene Township; pp. 555, Mill Creek; pp. 558-9, Elliott Chapel; pp. 638, William R. Boyd.

Hunt, W.E., Historical Collection of Coshocton County, Ohio, 1864–1876,Robert Clarke and Co, Printers, Cincinnati, Ohio, 1876, p. 208.

9. James Elliott, Oldest Son of John and Fanny Blaine Elliott lived in Holmes County.

JAMES ELLIOTT (1782–1849): oldest of the sons, James, Moses and Andrew and daughter, Mary stayed behind in Ireland. The three sons came in 1819 and the daughter Mary died in Ireland. (Lawrence, 1968) James Elliott was elected Coroner, Mechanic Township in 1832–1834, and Justice of the Peace, Mechanic Township 1829–32. His will was probated September 14, 1849 in Holmes County, Ohio. James Elliott was elected Coroner, Mechanic Township 1832–1834, Justice of the Peace Mechanic Township 1829–32. His will was probated September 14, 1849 in Holmes County, Ohio. The letter which follows was written by James Elliot(t) to his brother-in-law, Daniel Boyd and his wife (James' sister), Jane, from his farm:

Woodhill, dated 11th April 1842.

My dear Brother and Sister,

For the first time I believe in my life I write to you to inform you how we all are getting along. All our Families now are in tolerable good health except my Brother Thomas' Family. Lucy has been confined to her bed these many months but she has recovered so far that she bore to be removed to my Brother Sam's on last Friday and it was a great undertaking. She has had another boy (Thomas) about two weeks ago and considering her weak helpless condition the child seems to do well. Her mother has taken the baby (Thomas) and the other two youngest children(Newton and Nathan) home and the two oldest is with us (Simon and Daniel). Tom has sold his barn and lot for 800 dollars and his Father in Law has also sold and they all mean to start for the Ioway territory as soon as their health will permit which will be some time as Tom and all the Family was all so bad about a month ago that one could not give the other a drink but they are recovering fast. A great many has died with a complaint they call lung fever and the scarlet fever has also carried away a great many children and grown people. My son Tom got married on the 10th Feb to Mary, Williams Mott's Daughter, and lives in the house with us yet. They will take up for themselves after harvist. George David Elliot(t) and Richard _____James has rented his farm for two years and gets the _____half, We have 70 acres of wheat in this year and James 20 all of which looks well some of it, too well. So if we run? we will have a heavy harvist. Jamese's child is doing well but very troublesome. _____looks bad this child wore her down more than all the children she ever had. Your Brother Robert has rented your Brother Johns farm and has moved to it a few days ago. Wm. Dunkans Children had all the measles lately but they are recovering. My Mother is as well as she has been any time these 7 years. I intend going if alive and well to go to see you all in the fall and stay until you are tired of me. Eliza gets along finely and I believe quite contented. Edwards wife has got a fine boy he was nearly trampling us all under his feet when it was born. Uncle always asks him how his yellow boy comes on. I think he does not take it very well. Wheat is now 90 cents at Lewisville (Roscoe Village) we expect it will be a dollar when the boats will begin to run which will be next week. There never was such appearance of wheat in this neighborhood and a great dale (deal) of it sown. The family had a letter from their Brother he is near Bedford. He gives an account of Betty and Tom Anderson. Tom has signed the pledge as they call it and is doing better. It mentions Bill Walker which says he is doing well and out of debt but dont say anything about any one else except it would had saved me a great dale(deal) of trouble and my Brother _____ will have to do the same. I understand my Brother Andy is about settling out for 1000 dollars. We had a revival in our class at new years. 25 have joined among whom were old Bitney(?) and his son David and Eliza Jane _____ Caskey and his two sons and Daughter Wm. Dunk(an?) has also joined and George Elliot(t)'s Daughter Jane. Such a whillabalew(!) as we had you scarsely ever seen or heard. The temperance course is making great progress both in Holmes and Coshocton Counties. I have a barrel of good hard cider lying in the posnage? (parsonage) and no one goes near it. That mother whose child is "wearing her down" says its a fine thing she will soon have plenty of good vinegar. When George went to the seminary last May he got under conviction the first night and got through in two or three days. You won't think he was not the same person when he comes home. James thinks he must preach what is the reason he goes to the seminary, and the children made better? progress in learning. Beg to be remembered to every one of you and am my dear brother your very affectionate.

(signed) James Elliot(t)

10. Moses Elliott Family from Pennsylvania to Ohio to Missouri

Three of the older sons of John and Fanny Blaine Elliott (James, Moses and Andrew) stayed behind in Ireland; also a daughter, Mary, as well as two infants buried beside her husband. `The three sons came in 1819 and the daughter Mary died in Ireland. (Lawrence, 1968)

The elder Moses Elliott (1 Feb1784–19 Dec 1854), one of Fanny Blaine Elliott's older sons, brought his family to America in 1820. They settled first in Pennsylvania and after a few years moved to Athens Co., Ohio. The elder Moses was born February 1, 1784, in County Donegal, Ireland, came to the Pennsylvania in 1819 and settled as a farmer in Carthage Township, Athens County, Ohio in 1823. He lived on the farm where first settled, till his death in 1854. He was a justice of the peace for twelve years, and was highly respected as a citizen. His family, two sons, John and James plus five daughters were all living in 1869. (Walker, History of Athens County, 1869)

James Elliott, youngest son of Moses Elliott, was born in Carthage in 1826, and has lived ever since on the farm where he was born. He has been township clerk from many years and is held in high esteem in the community. (Walker, History of Athens County, 1869, pp.457)

John Elliott, the oldest son of Moses Elliott, born in Ireland in 1816, came to Carthage, Ohio with his father's family in 1823, and lived there until 1859. He was county commissioner several years and much esteemed. In 1859, he removed to Southwestern Missouri, where he still reside(s). During the Civil War he was driven from his farm on account of his Union sentiments, and was absent several years, but returned after the end of hostilities. (Walker, History of Athens County, 1869, pp. 457)

John's family, three sons, Koskioco, Moses and Charles plus five daughters, Mary, Alice, Ann, Sarah and Jane were all living in 1869. (Walker, History of Athens County, 1869) Their father was John Elliott (1816–1879), born 25 May 1816, County Donegal, Ireland; died 29 May 1879, Jasper County, Missouri. He is buried in the Webb City Cemetery. His wife was Charlotte Mansfield, born 28 September, Queen Anne County, Maryland; died 31 December 1883, Jasper County, Missouri. She is also buried in the Webb City Cemetery. The younger Moses Elliott is also buried in Webb City. His wife, Laura, was born in 1860. She, too, is buried in Webb City.

Koskioco Elliott was a surveyor of Jasper County, familiarly known as "Kos" Elliott, born in Athens County, Ohio, Oct. 23, 1843, moving from the old Ohio home at the age of fifteen with his father and family to Jasper County, near the post office of Sherwood.

At the beginning of the Civil War, the family returned to Ohio. Kos enlisted in 1864 in the One Hundred and Seventy-fourth Ohio, serving the remainder of the war. Kos married June 24, 1874, Linda L. Johns, a native of Mercer County, Ohio. Her birthday was Feb. 28, 1843. They have but one child, Mary L. Elliott. They lived on the farm formerly owned by the father of Mrs. Elliott, Mr. A. L. Johns, who was a pioneer in Iowa. Their farm of 150 acres was in sections 7 and 12, Township 29, Range 32 and 33, and had a small orchard besides other improvements. Kos was a member of the Grange and has been county surveyor for more than ten years, an office of no little responsibility and public service.

Linda L. Johns Elliott had attended school in a log schoolhouse where the city of Des Moines, Iowa stands today. Mrs. Elliott's father and mother, Mr. and Mrs. Johns, died on the home farm and are buried in the cemetery nearby called "Hoosier Point Cemetery," named from the point of timber near by the cemetery.

His uncle, Charles Elliott, DD, was for many years editor of the Western Christian Advocate and the Central Christian Advocate at another time, and later was president of the Wesleyan University of Iowa. He was also the author of "Elliott on Slavery" and History of the Great Secession of Methodism" in 1856, predicting the secession of the Southern states at no distant day. Kos had said that his father, John Elliott, was a native of Ireland, Killybegs, County Donegal, "where they eat potatoes, skins and all," who came to America in 1819, at the age of three years.

John Elliott was born in Killybegs, County Donegal, Ireland, on May 1, 1816, and came to America, locating first in Washington County, Pennsylvania, later removing to Athens County, Ohio, in the early days of its settlement. John Elliott remained in Ohio until 1859 coming to Jasper County, Missouri, and locating near Spring River, seven miles west of Carthage, and died on his farm there, in 1879.

Charlotta Mansfield, wife of John Elliott, was a daughter of Thomas Mansfield, who had been a soldier in the Revolutionary war, and his widow received a pension on that account. The Mansfield's came of an old and distinguished family of Maryland. They were parents of nine children who all grew to maturity.

Moses Elliott was one of the well-known old settlers of Jasper County, Missouri, since 1859. Moses Elliott resided on section 36, in Mineral Township. He was born in Athens County, Ohio, on February 4, 1849. Moses was ten years old when the family moved to Jasper County. He attended school, remaining with his parents until 1861. At that time, the whole family went back to Ohio and remained there until 1865, but then returned to Jasper County. He engaged in farming until 1875, when he went to Arizona and began mining. For the following five years he continued to mine, and then came back to his farm, in Jasper County. In 1885, he found the first lead on his land and began mining, while he continued farming.

In 1890, Mr. Elliott married Miss Laura Stults, who is a native of Springfield, Illinois, where she was reared and educate. She was the daughter of J.W. Stults, who was a native of Kentucky and one of the early settlers of Jasper County. Since 1896 Mr. Elliott has been a Democrat, and one of the best known among the early residents of the county.

The younger Moses and Laura Elliott raised Lora Elliott Storm(s). She also had a twin brother, Robert Lee Storm(s); a sister, Jeanette; a brother, Leslie; and another brother named Arthur. Addie Miller Storms died when Lora was eight years old and her father took her and her siblings to Washington State. She and her twin brother did not stay there very long. They came back to Missouri and her twin brother was raised by Robert Lee Storm(s)' brother, George Porter Storms and his wife Laura Bell Storm(s). Moses Elliott and Laura Stults Elliott raised Lora.

Linda L. Thompson, a g-g-g-g granddaughter, lives about 40 miles south of Kansas City, Missouri. She took up genealogy as a way to find out about family. She knew very little, and asked few questions as she grew from childhood and her parents died early in life or knew little about their own family history. Using library resources, she found information about her great uncles, Koskioc and Moses, and their move with their father, John Elliott (1816–1879), to Jasper Co., Missouri about the time of the Civil War. She found the Nathan Saunders Elliott web site, May 1998. Linda was the daughter of Robert Lee Storm(s) and Addie Miller. (Walker, History of Athens County, 1869, pp. 457)

11. Andrew Elliott lived in Ireland, Coshocton and Iowa

ANDREW ELLIOTT ((5 May 1790–13 May 1862) One of the older sons, (James, Moses and Andrew), who stayed behind in Ireland. The three sons came to Ohio in 1819. The daughter Mary died in Ireland. (Lawrence, 1968) Andrew and James married sisters in Ireland and through their wives were heir to a fortune in Ireland, but being Elliotts and unconcerned about wealth they never bothered to get the fortune (p. 15 Blanche Elliott, 1941).

In a letter to his sister, Samuel wrote that "Andrew sold his place for one thousand dollars and is bound for Missouri". (Samuel Elliott, in a letter dated June 16th 1842) Andrew must have traveled to Iowa to settle for a time, where his wife Anna S. Stevenson died and was buried at Quaspueton, Iowa. He returned to Coshocton County. Andrew lies buried in the Keene Methodist Cemetery next to his daughter Hester. The headstone carries both Andrew and Hester's date of death and age. Hester's husband, Albert Mansford, placed the headstone on the gravesite at a later date. Probably, both names were placed on the same stone as a measure of love and economy. Andrew married Ann S. Stevenson in Ireland in 1835.

Children: Hester (14 Jun 1836–7 Jul 1863) married Albert Mansford

ANNA S. STEVENSON married Andrew in 1835 when they took up farming as a way to make a living. They had a daughter, Hester, born in 1836. In 1842, they decided to head west for Missouri to seek their fortune. They journeyed to Quaspueton, Iowa, where Anna died and was buried in a local cemetery. Hester and her father returned to Keene, where she met and married, Albert Mansford. (ESE 11/17/93)

Quaspueton is located on the Wapsipincon River, about 25 miles east of Waterloo, Iowa. (Exit route 282 south from Interstate 20)

12. Charles Elliott, Methodist Minister lived in Pennsylvania, Ohio, Missouri, and Iowa.

CHARLES ELLIOTT (May 16, 1792–6 Jun 1869) Methodist preacher, editor and President of Iowa Wesleyan University. He lived in Cincinnati, Ohio, Mount Pleasant, Iowa, and other places. Charles, one of Frances Blaine's older sons, was one of the earlier circuit riders at Keene and elsewhere and became rather famous in Methodism throughout the Central West. He was a co-founder of Ohio Wesleyan as well as President of Iowa Wesleyan. He was editing a Methodist paper as well as teaching at the same time. Simon, a younger brother, was also a well known Methodist. Before Charles started out as an itinerant preacher, he and his younger brother George were schoolteachers in Keene, Clark, Mill Creek and Bethlehem Township schools. (Lawrence, 1968)

"In 1858 the trustees of Iowa Wesleyan elected as president the Rev. Charles Elliott, DD, LL.L. who had joined the faculty earlier as Professor of Ecclesiastical History and Biblical Literature. Previous presidents had been young men, beginning their careers, whereas Dr. Elliott was sixty-six years old and had achieved national Methodist distinction as a religious journalist and church historian.

Charles Elliott was born May 16 (or May 12), 1792 in Glenconway, Donegal County, Ireland, was converted to the Irish Wesleyan Society in 1811 and was licensed to preach in 1813. Since his religious affiliation prevented matriculation in the University of Dublin, he pursued a collegiate program of study independently. He came to the United States in 1814 and settled in Ohio where he was admitted to the Ohio Annual Conference of the M.E. Church in 1818 and assigned to the Zanesville Circuit. Charles Elliott lived in Uniontown prior to the time his mother and siblings came to the New World. He received ordination in the Methodist Church while he was still in Ireland (1813). Charles came to America in 1814 and was appointed Professor of Languages at Madison Academy in 1827. The earliest church organization in the Uniontown community was the Methodist Episcopal (1825). During those few years, he taught courses, recruited students, and ministered to the students in the school and people in the community. In 1828–29, under Charles Elliott, there was a great revival, which lasted through the summer and winter, and there were about one hundred and fifty accessions to the church. The revival swept all Uniontown and Madison College, and hundreds were converted. When Rev. H.B. Bascum resigned as president of Madison College in spring 1829, Professor J. H. Fielding and Rev. Charles Elliott were placed in charge. Charles Elliott was described as a pure and simple scholar who loved learning for its own sake. He and his family lived in a red frame house near the college taking in several boarders including his younger brother, Simon. In 1832, Madison College changed from support by the Methodist Conference and continued under the Cumberland Presbyterian Church until 1872 when it closed for lack of funds. As the change occurred, Charles moved on to Cincinnati and further success. Charles Elliott's brogue was pure Irish...he was said to have red hair. (Source: Frank R. Elliott, MD in Chicago, IL, great-grandson in a letter to Mrs. Jonasson, dated 8/9/67. Frank did not provide his lineage.)

In 1822 he spent a year as a missionary to the Wyandotte Indian Nation at Upper Sandusky, which he described in his book, Indian Missionary Reminiscences (1850), and in 1823 became Presiding Elder of the Ohio District. Turning to educational work, he served as Professor of Languages at Madison College, Uniontown, Pennsylvania from 1827–1831.

In 1828 and 1829, under Charles Elliot(t), there was a great revival, which lasted through the summer and winter, and there were about one hundred and fifty accessions to the church. This revival, under the same preacher, swept all Uniontown and Madison College, and hundreds were converted. This was said to have been the most remarkable revival of religion ever known in Uniontown, PA. (Ellis, Frank, History of Fayettee Co., Vol. 1–3, 688–689, 1882.)

This institution of the Pittsburgh Annual Conference later merged with Allegheny College and existed until 1872. From 1831–1833, Dr. Elliott was Presiding Elder of the Pittsburgh District. Here he began a long career in religious journalism as editor of the Pittsburgh Conference Journal 1833–1834 and the Western Christian Advocate 1836–1848. He was noted for his vigorous handling of controversial topics of church and national life.

He held churches in Springfield and Xenia, Ohio from 1848–1852 but returned to the editorial chair of the Western Christian Advocate 1852–1856. During these years he published the first of his many books, The Life of the Rev. Robert R. Roberts 1844, Delineation of Roman Catholicism 1841 and A History of the Great Secession From the Methodist Episcopal Church in the year 1855…"The Methodist Episcopal Church, South" 1855. The book on Romanism was for many decades a widely used polemic in American Protestant circles. The history of the formation of the Methodist Episcopal Church, South, although marked by Elliott's anti-slavery bias, is still a useful work of reference. His anti-slavery feelings were strongly expressed in the booklets, Slavery Contrary to the Spirit of Christianity and Sinfulness of American Slavery 1850.

In 1857, Dr. Elliott was invited by President Lucien W. Berry to join the faculty of Iowa Wesleyan University and founded the Biblical Department. From this position he became president in 1858, a position which he held until 1861 when he moved to St. Louis, Missouri as editor of the Central Christian Advocate, although he retained his professorship. Here he had a somewhat stormy career since Missouri was the dividing line of the two divisions of the Methodist Episcopal Church and of the slavery and anti-slavery regions. Frank C. Tucker has recounted these years in The Methodist Church in Missouri 1789–1939, published in 1966.

In 1863, Elliott returned to the Iowa Wesleyan presidency which he held until 1866 when ill health and age forced him to retire. He lived in Mount Pleasant until his death on January 6, 1869 and was buried in Forest Home Cemetery.

Charles Elliott's presidency was marked by the struggles to find funds for annual operations, the mortgage payment on Old Main and necessary building repairs. The Civil War caused a great fall off in student enrollments and when he took up the presidency again in 1863, he had to combine professorships to enable the school to survive. But Elliott did live to see a new influx of students in 1865 and the re-birth of college life and activity.

Dr. Elliott brought to Iowa Wesleyan a wider, more cosmopolitan touch than any previous president did. His national contacts were extremely wide and his name was known. Many details of his administration reveal his endeavor to bring the college into wider repute and sounder academic practice. He arranged for special ceremonies in 1859 when Lucy Webster Killpatrick was the first woman graduate; he designed an elaborate commencement program with a Latin title page in 1860; he opened a department of foreign languages with regular courses in French and German. This was made possible when he appointed to the faculty the Rev. Adam Miller, M.D., who had done pioneer work among German Methodists. Adam Miller's important book, Experiences of German Methodist Preachers was published in 1859 with a Mount Pleasant date line and to this Dr. Elliott contributed an introduction. Elliott likewise attracted to Mount Pleasant the retired Methodist Bishop, Leonidas L. Hamline for whom the Hamline Literary Society was named.

Dr. Elliott also presented for honorary degrees a number of important figures from the national scene: Benjamin F. Crary, President of Hamline University; Horatio N. Robinson, Professor of Mathematics at the United States Navel Academy; Robinson Scott, later a leading theologian of the Irish Wesleyan Church; Oliver M. Spencer, President of the State University of Iowa. Had Elliott been president at any other time than the Civil War period, his educational abilities would have created more rapid results. But he did exert upon the local scene an influence that was significant at the time. In his last years he published Southwestern Methodism, A History of the M.E. Church in the Southwest 1844 to 1864, 1868.

Dr. Elliott's connections continued with the university through his children. One daughter, Phoebe Leech Elliott was graduated in 1860; was Professor of English Literature and Preceptors 1864–1865 and served on the Board of Trustees from 1870–1875 while a resident of Mount Pleasant. A second daughter, Fannie, married the Rev. LeRoy Monroe Vernon of the class of 1860 who became superintendent of Methodist work in Italy 1871–1888. Vernon's daughter married an Italian poet, Angelo DeBossis, whose son Carlo DeBossis as a member of the Columbia University faculty visited Iowa Wesleyan in 1925.

Simon Charles Elliott, his son, married Francis Roads of the Class of 1869, who was one of the Seven Founders of the P.E.O. Sisterhood at Iowa Wesleyan. Francis Roads Elliott had an interesting career in art teaching and community service and biographical accounts appear in The History of the P.E.O. Sisterhood 1903 and in Winona Evans Reeves, The Story of P.E.O. 1869–1923. A memorial marker for her was placed on the Elliott family plot in the Forest Home Cemetery, Mount Pleasant, by the Supreme Chapter of the P.E.O Sisterhood in 1951." (L.S. Haselmayer, The Presidents, Iowa Wesleyan College, 1967)

Simon married _____ and had a daughter, Dorothy. She became one of the seven sisters of P.E.O., which originated at Mt. Pleasant, Iowa. She married twice, became Dorothy Canfield Fisher (Writer of Mystery). The Canfield family owned the Canfield Paper Co. in upstate New York.

Hadden, James. History of Uniontown, Pennsylvania, 1913. Reproduced by Unigrahic, In., 1978, pp. 490–492.
Ellis, Frank (Ed). History of Fayette County, PA., with Biographical Sketches of many of its Pioneers and Prominent Men. (Vol. 1–3), 1882, 315–316
(The Uniontown Public Library (1996) was a new building located near downtown, about a block from Route 40, and the center of town.)
Haselmayer, Louis A., Prof., Iowa Wesleyan College, The Presidents of Iowa Wesleyan College, 1967.

13. John Elliott, Rebel Son, Presbyterian and Builder of Local Churches

JOHN ELLIOTT (28 Mar 1795–2 Sep 1868) came to America with his family in 1816 at the age of 21. John was the brother called 'Rebel' John since he was the only Presbyterian in a long line of Methodist. He lived and died in Coshocton and was an elder in the Coshocton Mill Creek organization, which was the first Presbyterian organization in the County and started at Keene. He was a builder of churches, building both the first Presbyterian and the first Methodist in Coshocton. As a young man he had built mission houses among the Wyandotte in northern Ohio. (Lawrence, 1968)

"John built the first Presbyterian Church and first Methodist Church in Coshocton and many of the small churches about the County. Staunch Presbyterian that he was, he was always a contributor to the building fund of these churches whatever the denomination." Blanche Elliott, 1941, pp. 9.

Arlan Heiser (1999) has a copy of "Marriages Coshocton County, Ohio 1811–1993 Volume I". This lists the bride of John Elliott as Nancy Jane Blyth.

14. Samuel Elliott lived most of his life in Coshocton County

SAMUEL ELLIOTT (8 May 1800–12 Sep 1958) came to America in 1816 with the rest of the family. He was 16 years old at the time. He worked hard, bought land near his brother George, became a farmer, Justice of the Peace, Associate Judge, and a Methodist. For years, he lived as a neighbor to his brother, George, where Fannie made her home. His Justice of the Peace docket (1835–1845) demonstrated his fairness. He was elected an Associate Judge of Ohio and received his commission, January 10, 1846.

(Blanche Elliott, 1941). He was buried at Independence, Ohio, down river from Defiance.
Samuel married Sarah (Sally) Seward, 25 Oct 1825 in Clark Township, Coshocton County.

(Children: Elnor, Simon, Phobe Jane, Elisward, John Blaine, Albert, Nancy, Sarah, Samuel Wesley and Hester Ann.)

LETTER FROM SAMUEL ELLIOTT TO DANIEL BOYD

June 16th 1842
Clary (?) township

Dear Friends (Daniel and Jane Elliott Boyd)—

I write to you to let you know how we are all in reasonable health at present thanks to God for all his mercies both g (of) a spiritual and temporal nature. Thomas and family left Roscoe about the middle (of) April having sold his premises there in view of moving to the west in company with his father-I-law (and) his wife being sick at the same time she became confined to her bed about Christmas. In March she was delivered of a man child (Thomas) which is alive and doing very well. It is with a nurse, a daughter of (?) Cuniham which lost her child. They came to our house and after suffering extremely six weeks here she died in full and certain hope of blessed immortality. She was buried on Sunday the 22nd of May in Kenne her funeral was very large and a very feeling and interesting sermon was preached by the Rev. Mr. Beard of the Coshocton Circuit. He and his oldest child Simon and will remain until fall—(line illegible—Nuton (Newton) is at Alx. Finlays, Daniel at Brother James, Nathan at Nephew John Elliotts. He intends to go to the West this fall and make a purchasing of land and then return and set up shop in Coshocton.
We had a stranger present itself in our family on the 10th of February, which we name Nancy. I have entirely or nearly so lost the sight of my bad eye. It was ___?___ from a very slight hurt which very much ___?____me for several weeks but it is now so that it does not pain me any more. Nephew Thomas Elliott was married the to Mary Williams, daughter of Mathew Williams in the day our child was born. They have a fine boy which they name James (quicke work).
I want you to try and find where George Rickey lives in—(line illegible)—cort which will commence on the fourth of July and I would like to hear from you by that time or as soon after as you can make the necessary enquiries respecting Rickey. Will be obliqued to commence a suit against Rickey in your County if he does not comprimise if so I will pay you a visit I will not be _____to much thanks from you. Our wheats and oats crops here looks moderaly well. Corn's very backward and very much injured by the squirrals(?). Wheat is now down to seventy five cents at Roscoe and Coshocton. It rates at Massilon from ninety cents to one dollar. I took all my wheat to Massilon this last year and the greater part of the niborhood? goes there now from the advance price of wheat and the low price of goods. We do well in going. We make the trip in 2 1/2 and 3 days. We at best turn our time into money. John Boyd has rented his farm to Robert and gone to shoemaking to Keene. Andrew has sold his place for one

thousand dollars and is bound for Missouri. Church matters is in a deplorable situation on this Circuit and on some of the adjoining circuits and as nigh as I can bear wherever any of the comittee(?) travels who investigated the Allan affair this—and ministray? is doing no good. How great a matter's little fire kindereth on this circuit Br—?—had to expel 10 or fifteen from the names of _____so it appears the decision of the committee have ___ ____ _____ ____was expelled for illicit connexion with his niece. He had two trials before a commitee of the most prominent members of the circuit. From his first trial he appealed to the quarterly meeting and asked his case to be remanded back to the society for a new trial which ____ was granted by the quarterly conference. He has had the second trial and verdict come(to) the same as the first (quarterly). I (hear) that he has again appealed to quarterly conference. His name is Bradley—that he would let Coshocton County know that__Crawford and _ ___should not sit on Allen's trial __dealing has come down on his own fate however on this part of the circuit we live in peace and the preacher has had not trouble but west of Rocco and especially in the Allen nest (?) or we term it he has a hard row to hoe. Elder Powers popularity is forth (?) the decline exposity (?) among the people there is a case of slander pending before the cort of Common Please on Mount Union between him and a Mr. McNutty representative from Knox County.—(2 lines illegible)—McNutly expects to make good his expenses—on the whole. You have done well in getting out of the bounds of the North Ohio Conference. However, I think there is a goodly number of very worthy Ministers—such as McMahon___Linch and others. So much on the dark side of church matters but on the other side I have some news to say. In Coshocton the class numbers between 30 and 40 members and some of the richest and most influential men of the place such as of be C., Ricketts(?), Judge Schane (?) D Frew__ Old Mr. Rickets and Mr. Thomas is there leader. They are about building a meeting house. They have 12 or 13 hundred dollars subscribed therefore aburry(?) they will succeed without doubt.

Mother's (Fannie Blaine Elliott) health is as usual. She wishes to know when you (Daniel) and Jane will be to see her and wishes to be remebered to Moses and wife and family. Sarah joins me in her respects to you. I would very much like to make you a visit this fall if we could make it at all convenient but it runs every day and will bring it. Its our trouble and Implacement(?) that we have but little time or money to spare. The Allen affair cost us one hundred dollars in a fee to Old Mr. Silliman I _____myself and Brothers for they librally helped me. I do not ___or I have anything more to communicate only that we_____

Samuel Elliott (letter saved by Jane Elliott Boyd in a box, found years later, given to Roscoe Foundation and salvaged by volunteers. The letter was hard to read, written with homemade ink on local made paper.)

SARA H. SEWARD (17 Nov 1804–8 Aug 1891) and Samuel buried three infants: Eleanor (1833, 3 y 8m 19d), Eliza, and Ellse (16 Aug. 1837, 1y 7m) in the Keene Lower Methodist Cemetery. The families of George and Samuel were neighbors who rejoiced and sorrowed over their children together. Twice there were to be empty arms and aching hearts and Fannie was to see the dark hand of epidemic strike simultaneously at these two homes. George lost two small sons five days apart and within a few weeks Samuel lost a small daughter; and again, George lost a year-old son and Samuel lost a two-year-old daughter the next month.

15. Anne Elliott Shaffer Lived a Short Life

ANNE ELLIOTT (17 May 1802–16 Aug 1825) came to America with the rest of her family at the age of 14. She married Lyman Shaffer (7 Oct 1800–15 Nov 1871) on 8 May 1823. Lyman bought land from Thomas Elliott (Lot 66) in Millersburg in 1830. He and Margaret sold this lot in 1835. He worked as a tan-ner/farmer. Anne married and lived near Delaware, Ohio, until her early death (pp. 7, Blanche Elliott Essay, 1941). She died leaving a first-born infant. Her burial was in/near Delaware.

Lyman Shafer (1830 Census) Holmes Co., Hardy Township, page 288, Milesburg.

16. Jane Elliott Boyd Married Her Irish Sweetheart & lived in Coshocton and Athens Co.

JANE ELLIOTT BOYD (8 Apr 1803–4 Oct 1886). Jane lived in Coshocton County and Athens County. She married her Irish sweetheart who followed her to Ohio with his family. They raised a family of nine children. She was buried in Tuppers Plains Cemetery, Meigs County, near the Athens County line. Like her siblings, she came to America in 1816 with Fanny Blaine Elliott. "One of her children, Margaret, (known lovingly as Maggie) was the first woman graduate (1873) at Ohio University." (Source: Blanche Elliott, 1941, pp.9).

Ohio University built a woman's hall in 1913, and named it Margaret Boyd Hall.

The Methodist Cemetery in Tuppers Plains lies on the west side of the highway was you enter the village from the north. The church building was gone (1993) and the yard converted to business use. The cemetery appeared to be maintained only occasionally, and lay only partly visible from the highway. In the near side of the cemetery, headstones for each grave augmented the Boyd monuments. The main monument is cracked near the top. It has a basic information message about father Daniel, son John and daughter Mary Ann:

Married 8 Oct 1825 AT HOME, Doughty Creek, IN COSHOCTON (HOLMES) County.

(Children: John Elliott, Mary Ann, Jane, Katheryn, Hugh, Lucy A., William Fletcher, Fanny Blaine, and Margaret)

DANIEL BOYD (7 Sep 1794–20 Aug 1867). Daniel married Jane Elliott in 1825. He was living with his father, Robert, east of Keene on land which older folks of the 1960's generation knew as the Everett Boyd farm. Daniel came to America a year or more before his family, knowing that he would find his childhood sweetheart here in the 'Garden of Eden.' Daniel and Jane Elliott Boyd bought the farm just below Keene, which included all of the south part of the village and the original church site for the first Methodist church building. Courthouse records at Coshocton show the church deed written in 'goose quill' longhand from the Boyds to the Methodist Church in 1835, two acres for $50.

A history of Keene states that Daniel Boyd had a pet deer which followed him like a dog and would be seen at the store, which Richard, Daniel's' brother-in-law kept in the old Charlie Brenly house at the southwest corner of the cemetery. This was the first store in Keene. Daniel Boyd believed strongly in higher education so they did not stay long enough at Keene to see the first church built but moved down near Athens where eventually Margaret Boyd (1873) became the first woman to graduate from Ohio University, and Boyd Hall was named for her. Daniel himself, when he lived at Keene took a special course in Latin, walking back and forth to Coshocton each day. (Lawrence, 1968)

Daniel Boyd was born in Ireland in 1794, immigrated to the United States in 1819 and settled in Carthage Township as a farmer in 1838. He was an active member of the Methodist Church and an excellent citizen. He died on August 20, 1867. His oldest son, Dr John E. Boyd, died in West Virginia in 1855. His other two sons, Hugh and William F., graduated from the Ohio University in 1860 and 1866, respectively, and have engaged successfully in teaching. (Walker, History of Athens County, 1869, pp. 458)

Carthage Township lies just west of Troy Township, and the village of Coolville, Ohio.

LETTER WRITTEN BY D. BOYD, BUT PROBABLY NOT SENT TO NATHAN ELLIOTT.

Coolville March 28th 1865

Dear Nathan,

This is a wet day and I will write you a few lines myself. We received two letters from you yesterday, one to Mary Ann and one to Margaret. You say you are afraid you will never see the union as it was. Do not be discouraged. The union will be preserved and I hope you will live to see it done, and that you will have the honor of helping to do it. We had a letter from Johnson Boyd and one from George Boyd both yesterday. We were glad to hear that our relatives in the Army are all living and feel to thank Providence for their preservation so far and trust that they will be spared to the end of this wicked rebellion and return to their respective homes in safety. From some of your letters I was afraid your mind was getting bewildered on the subject of the war and the design of the emancipation proclamation. You seemed to think you were fighting to free slaves; that was a great mistake. Your business is to save the Union and let slavery take care of itself. And who is so blind as not to see that slavery was the great strength of the rebels and anything the government could do to weaken the rebellion was perfectly right and what business has a soldier to enquire whether a negro is better in a state of slavery or a state of freedom. It is strange indeed to hear of any one preferring to have negroes raising corn and pork for rebels while rebels are shooting down union men and striving to destroy the best government in the world. Again it is said you have turned democrat. Well, I have no objection to that if it be of the true Jefferson stamp, but if it is of that kind who sympathizes with rebels and do all they can to throw obstacles in the way of government I pity you. But I hope better things of you, and again there will be, or is now, union men. The balance of them will be butternuts or copperheads, and will be reckoned in the same category as Burr and Arnold, and I believe their children after them will share the disgrace of sympathizing with treason. And again, much as I long for your safe return and you have my poor prayers every day that God would preserve you yet I would rather hear of your bones bleaching on a southern battlefield than you to come home disgraced from the Army. But enough on this subject. Now for the news. A few deserters in Noble County and their Butternut friends said they would not return to the army and they would not be taken. One of the letters sent to the army encouraging desertion fell into the hands of a colonel. This was sent to governor Todd who ordered the arrest of the deserters. But the Copperheads to the number of 200 armed to resist. The Corporal and his men retired without giving all the details. Marshal Sands returned in a few days with two hundred armed soldiers and some mounted volunteers. The Butternuts got scared and by last accounts fourteen of the insurgents was arrested and doubtless will be dealt with according to their crimes. Fanny and Mag have written to you and I need not repeat what they have said. If I knowed you cared about papers I would send one occasionally. When you write tell us all you know of our friends in the army. Do you know anything of Andrew Duncan. Give my respects to Jeffers boys and D. Noyes, and again pray be hopeful and trustful and may the blessing of God be upon you.

Respectfully, Your Uncle Daniel Boyd

Athens County Marriages 1805–1865, Vol.1 np
Boyd, Daniel D. & Augusta C., One Hundred Years in America, 1820–1920, in custody of personal library of Marjorie Ward, Hilliard, Ohio, pg. 12, and Jeannette Gaskell Chevervenka, Boyd-Elliott-Eichhorn Connection, in custody of personal library of Nancy Leinweber, Euclid, OH, pg. 532 & 69–71.

17. Simon Elliott lived in Coshocton OH, Uniontown, Pennsylvania and Wellsville, Ohio

SIMON ELLIOTT (25 Oct 1809–24 Sep 1849) came to America with the family in 1816 at the age of seven. Simon became presiding Elder of Steubenville District in the Pittsburgh Conference at the time of his death. He was educated at Madison College, Uniontown, Pennsylvania under the supervision of his brother, Charles Elliott who was Professor of Literature at Madison College (1827–1831). He joined the Pittsburgh Conference in 1833 and held a number of leading positions in the Methodist Conference.
Simon Elliott's Will was recorded at Uttica, March 1, 1845, County of Fulton, State of Illinois. The court appointed John Elliot, son of John Elliott, and

Andrew Elliott, son of William Elliott to be executors. Simon wanted all my property equally divided between my brother's children. Rev. Simon Elliott is buried in the middle of a circle of Elliotts in the New Springfield Cemetery on top a bluff overlooking Wellsville, Ohio.

Simon married Christiani Groff on 8 Jun 1841 in Wellsville, Ohio.

CHRISTIANI GROFF ELLIOTT (1810–) In a letter from Mary Ann Boyd to her parents in Coolville (1849), she reported that her Uncle Simon had been in Keene and told her that his wife was not feeling well at all.

18. Thomas Elliott, Son of John and Fanny Blaine Elliott lived in Holmes County, Roscoe, and Coshocton, Ohio, Dawson, Illinois, and Guilford, Kansas.

Thomas (6 Aug 1807–1879?) came to Ohio with his family as a young boy (age nine). The family landed in the Inner Harbor, Baltimore, MD. They purchased a team and wagon to walk the National Road during the summer and fall of 1816. The wooden shipping box that carried most of Thomas's goods was handed down through the generations to Virginia Stevens. She wrote (9/90) that she has an emigrate chest that the Elliott family brought over from Europe. It is something to see! 2 ft. wide, 4 ft. long and about 3 ft. high. Big metal handles on each end. The family prided their walk to Ohio by saying they forded every stream on the way without help, except for the float across the Ohio River. Frances Blaine Elliott led nine of her children to land purchased in Mill Creek Township (organized in 1817) where the Elliott family lived when first they arrived in Ohio.

In the 1820's, the Nathan Saunders II family located in Millersburg, Ohio. Thomas Elliott married daughter, Lucy, in 1832. Lucy died in the spring of 1842 as they were making plans to go west with Nathan Saunders' extended family. Lucy was weak after giving birth to her fifth son earlier in the spring. She died in May from Lung Fever. Nathan Saunders left Ohio in the fall of 1842. He took his family to the Iowa Territory. The family planned to head for California in early Spring of 1843 with Thomas Elliott, who planned to place his boys with relatives while he went west for a year or so. His brothers, Samuel and George, convinced him to stay in Ohio with his five boys.

In 1870, Thomas Elliott again became a pioneer who helped settle Kansas. He was an assistant Pastor, Methodist Church, sponsored by his congregation in Dawson, Illinois, to help build a church building in Guilford. Town leaders expected the county seat to be located in the geographic center of the County, but it never happened. The completed building was used as a school for many years, and finally taken down in the early '20s. "Rev, Elliot is getting the material on the ground for a large business house, to be erected on State Street, nearly opposite Morse's store." (Guilford Citizen, May 28, 1870) "Rev. Thomas Elliott, who is superintending the building of the M.E. Church at this place, and who is the chief architect, is progressing finely, and will soon have the body of it up." (Guilford Citizen, Aug. 20, 1870)

In 1874, Thomas wrote to his older brother George living in Coshocton County that his second wife, Nancy thought he was partial to first wife, Lucy's, children. Nancy felt her children were being left out. The Kansas Census of 1875 listed Thomas Elliott age 68, occupation as wagon maker, born in Ireland, where from to Kansas was Illinois, living in Cowly, Wilson County, in Verdigris Township (Vol. 611, p. 24).
—Wilson County Citizen and Guilford Citizen, published April 21, 1870, Guilford, Kansas until Vol. 1: 27, then moved to Neodasha, Kansas, May 28, 1870 and August 20, 1870.

19. Thomas Elliott and second wife, Nancy Nutt

Thomas (1807–1879?) married a second wife, Nancy Nutt (1810–1870?) in 1844 in Coshocton, Ohio. They had four children, but Thomas favored the children of his first marriage. Thomas and Nancy did not get along well. The children were: Charles H. (1845–1930), David S. (1847–1912), Napoleon B. (1849–1852), and Lucy (1856–1933). One of their sons, Charles H. moved from Ohio to Winfield, Kansas, raised a family and lost track of other relatives. From time to time, some descendants of Nathan Saunders Elliott heard about their family, but they never seemed to touch each other. Then, in 1998, a g-g-g-grand daughter decided to try the Internet to search for relatives.

Nancy Elliott Harvey connected with Elaine Elliott through a request for information on the Internet. She and her family live in Zanesville, OH. Her father, Rodney D. Elliott, taught at Ohio University for 30 years. On occasion, they visited Roscoe Village and many of the Elliott family sites. Nancy found the writing of Blanche Elliott concerning Fanny Blaine Elliott in the Public Library in Coshocton. She believed that Elliott cousins were around, but they always missed connecting. They connected, August 1998.

Unpublished family information, E.S. Elliott, 1984. Thomas married Nancy Nutt in Coshocton in 1844. Their marriage is recorded in Coshocton Public Records.

20. Simon Elliott, oldest son of Thomas Elliott

SIMON ELLIOTT (15 Dec 1832–1877?) Simon was the oldest of 5 boys. He was named for his Uncle Simon, younger brother of Thomas. He was born in Millersburg, Holmes County, Ohio, December 15, 1832. Until about the age of sixteen he attended school and worked with his father in the wagon shop. He then began the molder's trade in the foundry at Roscoe, and remained there about two years. He went to Walhonding in 1848, remained until the year 1864, and the next spring went to Kansas, where he followed farming.

About 1865, he lived near Wetmore, Kansas, on the Potowatomie Indian Reservation. Until about the age of 16, he attended school and worked in his father's wagon shop. He learned the molder's trade in Roscoe, moved to Walhonding, where he met his wife and remained there until 1864. They moved to Kansas in 1865. They had one son, Edward L., born 25 August 1866. They farmed for 14 years, and returned home because of his wife's ill health. He returned to Coshocton County, Jefferson Township, where he died and was buried. (pp 674, History of Coshocton County, Biographical Sketches, 1881) In 1875–77, Simon operated a foundry on the basement floor of a three-story general repair shop to the right of the Walhonding bridge in the village of Warsaw (pp 519–520)

Electra (1835–1875) was the daughter of Allen and Margaret (Smith) Butler. Their son, Edward L. was born, August 25, 1866, in the Osage Indian Reserve, in Kansas. (Pp. 674, History of Coshocton County, Biographical Sketches, 1881)

21. Daniel Gross Elliott–second son of Thomas Elliott lived in Ohio and Missouri.

DANIEL GROSS ELLIOTT (21 Sep 1834–20 Feb 1912) was the second-born of five boys of Thomas and Lucy Saunders Elliott. He was named for the husband of her older sister, Sarah. When Daniel's mother died, the older boys,

Simon and Daniel went to live with George or James Elliott. Daniel was on his own by the time he was sixteen years old (1854).

Daniel married Catherine Henderson in 1855. He was drafted for military service during the Civil War in 1862. His complexion was florid, eyes gray, hair red, and by occupation a machinist. He was 5 ft. 9 1/2 in tall and 28 years old when he reported to Camp Zanesville, Ohio, Sep. 1, 1862. The bounty paid for his enlistment was $25 dollars and a premium of $2. When he joined for duty for three years, he was appointed corporal. August 5, at Walhonding, Ohio, and promoted 4Sergt. (Dec 26, 1862) Co. H., 97th Reg't Ohio Infantry. He was issued one haversack and 1 canteen (Sept. 1863), and ordered to Columbus, Ohio, after drafted men by Major Ben. Thomas. He was on detached duty for recruiting service, Army of the Cumberland, headquarters, per S.F.O. 48, dated Feb. 17, 1864. He was mustered out in compliance with a telegram from the War Dept., dated May 18/29, 1865. (mustered out on individual roll June 15, 1865). He was a patient on the Hospital Muster Roll, No. 8, U.S.A. General Hospital, Nashville, Tenn., in July and August 1864. He was reported present and died Sep. 6., 1864. according to J. Castie, copyist. He had remittent fever, but lived on until 1912. (Source: Veterans Records, National Archives, Washington, D.C.)

After the Civil War, Daniel moved to South Central Missouri, took up farming near Houston, Missouri and lived out his life. He was pictured with Nathan and Simon Elliott in a turn-of-the-century picture, but no one is sure where or when the picture was taken. Daniel was the proprietor of the Elliott Foundry, established in 1875. Its original dimensions were 20 X 40 feet, and was run by horsepower, but became a much larger building, fitted with the best machinery—a twelve-horsepower engine. His ironwork was done during the summer and woodwork, during the winter season. In the beginning, he owned 20 acres and expanded to 206 acres. He learned his trade from his father, Thomas, working in his father's wagon and general machine shop in Millersburg at twelve years of age. By age sixteen, he commanded a journeyman's wage.

In 1853, he engaged in his father's old stand, where he remained until 1862, then enlisted in Co. H, of the Ninety-Seventh Infantry, and served as orderly sergeant until May 15, 1865. After the war, he resumed business at the old stand until the spring of 1867, when he located on a farm in Texas County, Missouri, but soon began work as a carpenter and mechanic. He was a member of the Methodist

Episcopal Church, the GAR and a Republican. (From History of Missouri, 1889, complied by Goodspeed including a History of Texas County)

Daniel Gross Elliott's (1834–1912) g-g-g-granddaughter, Elaine Elliott lives in California and learned to use a computer in her business. She returns to the Ozarks of Missouri occasionally to visit family. She checked a web site entitled rootsweb that included a listing of Missouri Pioneers. Several weeks earlier, Earl S. Elliott placed several Missouri Pioneer names on the web-page hoping to find a distant cousin who knew something about the Daniel Gross Elliott family. Back in California, Elaine found the David Gross Elliott name on a web page of Missouri Pioneers and tried to contact the sender, but ESE was out of town and changed his address from AOL to PSU. Time passed (about six months), before ESE got around to upgrading his address on the web page. Bang! The next day, ESE received a request for information about Daniel Gross Elliott and the Elliott family. A firm Internet connection followed with Elaine and her father supplying information about their family and gaining Elliott family information about the whole family. Some Shipman/Elliott descendants lived in the Ozarks as children and vaguely remembered a Mortuary in Texas County, Mo. operated by an Elliott family.

Elliott, Daniel G., U.S. Military Service Record, 1861–1865. Veterans Records, National Archives, Washington, D.C.

History of Missouri, 1889, Goodspeed including a History of Texas County. Hayward L. Elliott gathered family history with his daughter, Elaine Elliott. They have family records and pictures that date to 1998.

22. Nathan Saunders, third son of Thomas Elliott lived in Ohio, Illinois and Missouri

NATHAN S. ELLIOTT (1 Feb 1841–28 Jun 1915) was the third son (Simon, Daniel Gross, Nathan and Thomas) of Thomas (1807–1879?) and Lucy Saunders Elliott (1812–18 May 1842). He was born in Roscoe Village, near Coshocton, Ohio. His father was working as a wheelwright. The village is located on the west bank of the Muskingum/Tuscorowas rivers. Parts of the canal were restored along with the restoration of Roscoe Village in the 1970's. He was named for his maternal grandfather, Nathan Saunders. Within 18 months, he and his brothers lost their mother, Lucy. She died around May 20 and was buried, Sunday, May

22, 1842. She was buried in the Methodist Cemetery in Keene near other members of the Elliott family. In 1844, father Thomas married Nancy Nutt (1825?–1870?) and added three children more to his brood. Who assumed the care and raising of the surviving Saunders boys seems to be a family matter that is not clear. Nathan may have learned the carpentry trade from his father. However, he spent a part of his childhood and youth living with his Aunt Jane and her family in Coolville, Ohio.

At the time the Civil War broke out, Nathan was living in Coolville, Athens County. He volunteered for the 53rd Regiment of the Ohio Infantry Volunteers; Company B. He joined for three years, at age twenty, as a private on October 5, 1861, at Camp Diamond, Ohio, near Jackson, in Athens County. According to his record and military history, October 5 through December 31, 1861, was the basic training period for the regiment, i.e., about ninety days. Nathan was appointed 2nd Corporal on November 2, and issued a Springfield rifled musket along with other members of Co. A and B, while the other Co. received older musket loaders, i.e. Austrian or French. At the time of his enlistment, and according to his record, he was six feet, one inch tall, had blue eyes, dark hair and by occupation, a carpenter. The only comment on his enlistment record was the name: Miss Mary A. Boyd (single), Coolville, Athens, County, Ohio. The custom was to name someone to notify in case of emergency or death. One could speculate that she was a girlfriend that Nathan met while training at Camp Diamond. More likely, the Boyds were related, and she was a "kissin' cousin."

The 53rd volunteer infantry regiment (OVI) was organized at Camp Diamond, Jackson, Ohio, from October 5, 1861, to February 5, 1862. ®7 The original members (except veterans) were mustered out October 3, 1864, by reason of expiration of term of service. The regiment was mustered out of service August 11, 1865, at Little Rock, Arkansas, in accordance with orders from the War Department. The official list of battles included seventeen locations beginning with Shiloh in Tennessee in early April 1862, and ending with the North Edisto River in South Carolina, in February 1865. The regiment was part of the 15th Army Corps (Army of the Tennessee) commanded by U.S. Grant until promoted to higher command, then W.T. Sherman who commanded three Corps, then J. McPherson who was killed at the Battle of Atlanta, and finally O.O. Howard. The 53rd was part of the 5th Division, until the Battle for Atlanta, then assigned to the 2nd Division under M. L. Smith, and 2nd Brigade under J. A. J. Lightburn, later commanded by their former regimental commander, W. S. Jones. During active service, the 53rd was commanded by (1) J. Appler who was forced to resign after Shiloh, then (2) W. S. Jones who was later promoted to Brigade commander, and (3) R. A. Fulton who remained with the Regiment until discharged December 11, 1864. The regiment marched through Tennessee, Mississippi, Alabama, Georgia and both Carolinas. In 1862, near the beginning of the western conflict in the Tennessee area, Grant was appointed commander of the Army of Western Tennessee, with Sherman and others under his command. In the fall of 1963, shortly after the Battle of Chickamauga and before the Battle of Chattanooga, Lincoln decided to consolidate the western command with Grant in charge of all Union troops. The command was composed of three armies. The largest was the Army of the Cumberland under Thomas, while the Army of the Ohio under Schofield the smallest, and the Army of the Tennessee was the third unit. Nathan traveled in eight states with the Army of Tennessee, roughly composed of seventy-one regiments, or 30,000 officers and men. Their commanding officer was (1) Wm. T. Sherman, until promoted, followed by (2) James B. McPherson until he was killed at Atlanta and then by (3) W.S. Jones. At the end of the conflict, the 53rd OVI was part of the Second Division, Fifteenth Army Corp. The Regiment traveled 6400 miles, engaged in sixty-seven battles and skirmishes, had sixty officers and men killed, and two hundred and sixty-four officers and men wounded. Unfortunately, the 53rd was badly embarrassed at Shiloh, when attacking Confederate units overran them. On the positive side, their major successful campaigns included the Campaign for Vicksburg (Sherman's men faced defeat at Chickasaw Bluff while the 53rd was chasing Van Dorn near Holly Springs, Miss., and were later transported to Haines Bluff where they joined a march to the Big Black River to frustrate Johnson's effort to relieve Vicksburg) and the battle over Missionary Ridge, near Chattanooga, Tenn. Other major campaigns included the march through Georgia during the Atlanta Campaign and the march to the sea and capture of Savannah in 1864. The winter campaign of '65 through South and North Carolina finally ended in the victory parade through Washington, D.C.

Nathan rose through the enlisted ranks during his enlistment. He made 3rd Sergeant, November 1, 1862, and re-enlisted at age 22 in Scottsboro, Alabama, June 1, 1864. At that time, the 53rd was closing their winter camp and preparing for the assault on Atlanta. Enlistment of veterans was a growing concern for the Federals. In late May, Sherman was trying to outflank Joe Johnston's Confederate units during the battle for Dallas, Ga. For the next hundred days, the armies were on the move in constant contact with the enemy, and never had opportunity to sleep easy, prepare meals, or take a bath. For the most part, the three armies shifted from end to end in order to outflank Johnston's defenses.

At Kennesaw Mountain, the 53rd was part of a direct assault with hand-to-hand combat on Little Kennesaw Mountain that failed to break the rebel line. In September 1864, Nathan was promoted to 1st Sergeant after the capture of Atlanta. On May 20, 1865, as the war ended, he was commissioned a 1st Lieutenant and stayed with Co. B until discharged on the 11th day of August 1865 in Little Rock Arkansas. ®50 In January, February and March of '63, Nathan's outfit had a month's furlough. They boarded a northbound train on the evening of January 25th, 1864, headed for Nashville, homeward bound on a veteran's furlough. They reached Nashville on the 27th, then traveled to Cincinnati, Ohio where they reformed on March 12 in order to return to Scottsboro, Ala., their winter quarters. Nathan probably stayed in Nashville, Tenn. to visit his brother (Thomas) who was recovering from wounds received at Chickamauga.

Following his discharge from the army of occupation in Arkansas (August 1865), Nathan journeyed north to visit his father in Ohio or more likely Illinois. Meanwhile, his younger brother Thomas met and married his Illinois wife while recovering from his war wounds in Nashville. Nathan came to visit them in Illinois and stayed in Sangamon County to marry Martha Mallicent Yates (1845–1881) on March 28, 1867, near Berlin, Illinois. Martha gave birth to two children, Ira Elliott, born December 12, 1869, and Lillie C. Elliott, born June 20, 1871. The family lived in Illinois for about six years, 1865–1871, then moved west to Iowa briefly and on to Craig, Missouri in 1877. Nathan took up the carpentry business. He built their home at 203 Main St. where Martha died early in the winter of 1881. She was probably buried in a local cemetery, near Craig, but we have no record.

In June 1884, Nathan, who was now 43 years of age, climbed down into the well on their property to clean it out. When he came out of the well, the cold water had chilled his legs, and they gave way. He was unable to work for three months, and his legs gave him trouble for the rest of his life. During this time, he met and married his second wife, Ardilla Lee Redmon (12 Jul. 1863–22 Feb. 1916). They married December 20, 1885. William Redmon, her father, lived in Holt County, and probably farmed near Craig. "Ardie Lee" was a life-long resident of Craig and had known Nathan for some time. Their five children, born in Craig, were Earl Saunders (3 Dec 1887–14 Jul. 1944), Benjamin Franklin (14 Jan 1891–28 Aug.

1944), Charles Metz (6 Jun 1896–24 Jun 1951), Grace Maxine (31 Oct. 1898–16 Jul. 1961) and Ruth Isabella (1 Apr. 1901–28 Aug. 1975).

The family lived in Craig until 1904. During his later years, Nathan tried lumber dealing as a way to make a living, and traveled to the Ozarks where the boys helped haul lumber on Elliott Hill. They lived out their lives in northwest Missouri, except for two years when they moved to Winona (1905–07), a southern Missouri town in Shannon County; He applied for a veteran's pension in March 16, 1907, (age 65). The medical board reviewed his case and indicated that he had varicose veins in both legs. In due time his petition was approved. After Ardilla Lee broke her leg early in 1908, they returned to Rushville, near St. Joseph. With declining health, Nathan lived to age 74, and died June 28, 1915. Ardilla applied for widow and child benefits, since Ruth, the youngest child, was less than sixteen years of age. Ardilla Lee lived on for only six months.

Earl became Ruth's guardian, when their mother, Ardilla Lee, died, February 22, 1916. In the application papers, Eva Redmon Burke and her husband signed as witnesses. Eva was a sister of Ardilla Lee who lived in St. Joseph at the time. The marriage license for Nathan and Ardilla Lee (Arda) was filed in the County Court House in Oregon, Missouri, Holt County. Elizabeth Elliott gave (18 Nov. 1962) a set of veteran papers of Nathan S. Elliot to Grace Miller so that application for a military grave head stone could be documented.

Official Roster of the Soldiers of the State of Ohio in the War of the Rebellion, 1861–1865. No. L. IV: 37ᵗʰ–53ʳᵈ Regiments—Infantry, the Authority of the General Assembly, Werner PTG and MFG Co., 1887, 44 (673)
Elliott, Nathan S., U.S. Military Service Record and Veterans Benefits application 1861–1865, 1890, 1901, 1907, 1915, 1916.
Duke, John K., History of the Fifty-Third Regiment Ohio Volunteer Infantry, during the War of the Rebellion, 1861 TO 1865. Bland Printing Co., Portsmith, Ohio, 1900.
Elliott, Earl S. Jr. "Three Days at Shiloh". Unpublished manuscript on the 53ʳᵈ OVI at the Battle of Shiloh, 64 pp., 1994.
Elliott, Earl S., Jr. "Vicksburg to Chattanooga, Atlanta, Savannah and the Winter Carolinas March." Unpublished manuscript on the Campaigns of the 53ʳᵈ OVI and the XV CORPS in the American Civil War, 1861–1865. 123 pp., 1996.

23. Martha Mallicent Yates, first wife of Nathan S. Elliott, lived in Illinois and Missouri.

MARTHA M. YATES (11 Jun 1845–20 Dec 1881) After Nathan was discharged from the service, he returned North to visit his father in Ohio or more likely Illinois. He stayed in Sangamon County to marry Martha Mallicent Yates (1845–1881) on March 28, 1867, near Berlin, Illinois. They had two children, Ira Elliott, born December 12, 1869, and Cora "Lillie" Lillian Elliott, born June 20, 1871. The family lived in Illinois for about six years, 1865–1871, then moved west to Iowa briefly, and on to Craig, Missouri. They arrived in Craig, 1 August 1877. Martha died during the winter of 1881. She was one of ten children.

Her father, Thomas (14 Mar, 1811) was born in Gallatin County, Kentucky, was married 29 Mar 1837, in Berlin, Illinois to Nancy Higgins, (23 May 1816) who came with her parents to Sangamon County in 1836 (She died 15 Dec, 1860). (Living Descendants of Early Settlers of Sagamon County) The family was related to Richard Yates who was elected Governor of Illinois in 1856 (Civil War), and her Great Uncle was John Marshall (U.S. Supreme Court Judge). They lived in Island Groove Township outside of Springfield. Thomas farmed 600 acres.

Inman, Benjamin, grandson of Cora "LILLIE" Lillian Elliott, letters and telephone conversations, 1994–1996.

24. Families of Ira Yates Elliott & Children, Cecil, Willis and Ira, Jr.

IRA ELLIOTT (12 Nov 1869–1 Jan 1953) called "Y" by family members, was the oldest son of Nathan Saunders Elliott and Martha M. Yates born in New Berlin, Illinois. They lived in Sagamon County, Berlin Township, State of Illinois for seven years, then moved with the family by wagon to Craig, Missouri, and lived out his life in Northwest Missouri. He worked from youth as a railroad telegrapher. He was the member of the family who kept in touch with the families of children and grandchildren. He worked on the Burlington railroad for over thirty years, and later became an orchard farmer near Rushville. He lived to be eighty-four years old.

Ira learned telegraphy in Craig, Missouri and worked for the Burlington Railroad in Rushville, Missouri and also Leavenworth, Kansas. He spoke of walking to work across the ice on the Missouri River to the East Leavenworth, Kansas depot. He was a railroad agent earning low wages and working twelve hours a day, seven days a week, where he managed company business handling freight and passenger tickets. Each day there were five Burlington passenger trains each way between St. Joseph and Kansas City, and two Santa Fe trains each way between St. Joseph and Topeka, Kansas. The Rock Island had a mixed train between St. Joseph and Edgerton Junction. During the depression of the 1930's, Papa was still working on some farm project and made loans to farmers for the St. Louis Missouri Farm Land Bank. He managed to visit Ira, Jr. on weekends, enjoyed going to the Independence Boulevard Christian Church and tried to attend each weekend. "Say, by the way…" was a common phrase of Ira. He traveled with a small black railroad valise, a railroad watch, a collarless shirt, a dark suit, and a stiff straw hat with a 3" rim. He flagged a train as needed for his travel, so he came and went with little fanfare or advance notice. (Carl Miller, 1994)

Fannie Lay (8 Feb 1871–6 Aug 1907) traces her family back to Scott County, Virginia and North Carolina in the 1790's. She passed away rather suddenly after giving life to three boys; i.e. Cecil was fifteen, Willis was eleven and Ira, Jr. was nine when she died. Her brother, Pat was an engineer on a railroad. The train engine exploded and he was severely scalded. He died. Mamma was pregnant at the time. She went into labor and died in the St. Joseph Hospital, St. Joseph, Missouri, Aug 6, 1907.

Ira did keep the children and tried to keep a housekeeper, sometimes a married couple or a cousin, but many times they bachelored. He did the best he could, so they were a close knit and loyal family. People in Rushville gave them lots of support. Burial: ARMSTRONG CEMETERY

Elliott, Dorothy Talbert, Unpublished reports, letters and conversations regarding the Elliott/Yates family, 1994–1996.

25. Manasa P. Lay—Missouri Brigade, Confederate States, lived in Missouri.

Manasa P. Lay (14 Jul 1830–15 Dec 1908) is buried in the family plot located in lower part of the Rushville cemetery. He served with the Confederacy during the War Between the States with Elijah Gate's Missouri regiment. He enlisted October 30, 1862, at Camp Bragg by Captain Quesenberry for a period of three years during the war. The Missouri Brigade served from Pea Ridge to Franklin.

Nathan Saunders Elliott served with the 53rd OVI at Kennesaw Mountain while Manasa P. Lay served with the Missouri Brigade on the ridge overlooking the Union forces. At Kennesaw Mountain, the 53rd was part of a direct assault with hand-to-hand combat on Little Kennesaw Mountain that failed to break the rebel line.

Elliott, Dorothy Talbert, wife of Ira, Jr., conversations and letters regarding the Martha Malicent Yates Elliott family, 1994.

26. Families of Cora Lillian "Lilly" Elliott Inman

CORA "LILLIE" LILLIAN ELLIOTT (20 Jun 1871–4 Jun 1941) took a trip west to see Oregon and Washington and stayed to marry Ben Inman on Christmas Day, 1889. They got into the pure breed business, raising Brown Swiss Cattle. They also raised two of their own children and adopted two more.
Lillie wrote a letter from Junction City, Oregon, dated Feb 12th 1911 to Ira Elliott Jr. about his trip back home after spending the summer with them. She was looking forward to having the other boys come out west and visit for a summer. Lillie sent a letter (12/27/39) including several copies of their 50th wedding anniversary picture to Grace Miller. The Inman's celebrated their Golden Wedding Anniversary, December 25, 1939. She wrote indicating that she was "quite a lot better, but not able to do my work yet". The folder contained a copy of their wedding picture (1889) and their 50th anniversary (1939) picture. Moses D. Evers wrote a poem celebrating the event. (Copy received from Virginia Stevens 10/90, she found the dedication among memento's collected by her mother, Ruth Elliott (Mom saved everything). They had three (one son was killed at age sixteen) children of their own and two foster children.

Benjamin Price Inman was born in the Inman Home at Elmira, October 19, 1865. The Inman farm is a "Century Farm" and the "Inman Cemetery" which is one of the oldest cemeteries in the area is on this farm. BP was a breeder of Brown Swiss Cattle. He was a resident of Oregon that Lillie met on a trip west. BP & Lillie were married on Christmas day, 1889. According to EC Elliott notes, their children were girls. (Incorrect) They had one boy, Ira Murrell, and one girl, Barbara Virle, of their own and raised two children, Holley Leroy & Mary Gay, whom they adopted. Ben and Lillian were married at the home of Uncle Havey Yates in Elmira, Oregon. They had one son, Ira Maurell Inman and one daughter, Barbara Virle Inman. The also had a foster daughter, Mary Gay and a foster son, Holley Leroy Jarvis. Ira Murrell Inman had two sons, Ben and Richard. Barbara Virle Inman Lewis had one son, Own Alvin Lewis. He was electrocuted at age sixteen while operating a movie projector. They lived in Haines, Alaska at the time. He is buried in the Inman Cemetery at Elmira, Oregon. He was Ben and Lillian's grandson. (Ben Inman, May 29, 1996)

Inman, Robert D., born in Miami County, Ohio, August 11, 1853. His parents were Asa and Lucinda (Kendall) Inman. He went overland to Oregon in the 1865 Company led by William Davidson. Robert married Frances L. Guild in 1875. They had two children. (SOURCE: reported in Portrait & Biographical Record of the Willamette Valley, Oregon. Chapman Publishing Co., Chicago, Ill., 1903.)

Elliott, Dorothy Talbert, Unpublished reports, letters and conversations regarding the Elliott/Yates family, 1994–1996.
Inman, Benjamin P, grandson. Unpublished reports, family history and letters regarding the Inman family, 1994–1996.

27. Elliott, Thomas—son of Thomas Elliott lived in Ohio and Illinois.

THOMAS ELLIOTT (25 Mar 1842–14 Mar 1899) was the youngest of five brothers. He was born in 1842, as his mother lay weakened by a flu-like infection. She died about six weeks after he was born. He was cared for by family members until he reached the age of majority (age sixteen) when he went to work on his own. He joined the 51st OVI at Spring Mountain as a private when he was 18 years old. The regiment was composed mostly of Coshocton County boys.

The history of the 51st OVI was included in the History of Coshocton County, Ohio, published by A.A. GRAHM & CO., Newark Ohio, 1881, PP, 337–344. Thomas was listed as a private in Company I. As mentioned above, the 51st OVI was composed of many boys from Coshocton County. Thomas joined the 51st OVI, Company I, for three years at Spring Mountain, Ohio, Sept 18, 1861, as a private, by J.M. Crooks. When he volunteered for the OVI, he was nineteen years old, 5ft. 7 in. in height, had light complexion, eyes were blue, and hair dark. He was detached as a Division teamster, Camp Wickliffer, KY, Jan 7, 1862, by order of Gen. Nelson. In May-Aug, he was temporarily detached for service in artillery. Later, he was wounded in action at the Battle of Munfreesboro (Dec. 30–Jan 3) on Stones River, Tennessee, Jan 2, 1863. (Source: Report of Gen. Rosencrans, pp. 498) He was wounded in the left thigh and a patient in the Hospital at Covington, Kentucky and Camp Dennison, Ohio. He rejoined his outfit for duty May 25, 1863. On Sept 19, 1863, he was missing in action at Chickamauga, and later reported wounded in the right side on the casualty sheet. He was on the Hospital Muster Roll at Nashville, Tennessee and Covington, Kentucky, through a large part of his remaining enlistment. He was mustered out near Vilanow, Georgia, Oct. 17, 1864, when his clothing account was settled with a money advance of $78.41. He received $100 due, subsistence and transportation to Nashville, Tenn. when he was discharged by reason of expiration of terms of service. (Source: Veterans Records, National Archives, Washington, and D.C.)

He moved to Berlin, Ill. after the war, raised a family in Dawson, Illinois and died there in 1899. In 1975, Earl Elliott, Jr. found a voter registration record (dated Oct. 17, 1865) in the Clayville coach stop, about two miles east from Pleasant Plains, and west of Springfield, Illinois, while visiting the restored building. The register listed Thomas Elliott, as living in Berlin, ten miles west of Springfield, off the old Jacksonville road. At that time, he lived in Cartwright Township (formerly Island Groove), Sangamon County.
Thomas married Sarah Dawson (26 June 1865) and moved to Dawson, Illinois where he farmed until his death in 1899. (Children: Etta B, William Arthur, and Minnie Elizabeth)

BATTLE OF Chickamauga (19 SEP 1863), 14TH CORPS—THOMAS: 3RD DIV—VAN CLEVE: 3RD BRIGADE—BARNES: 51TH OVI—McCLAIN/ WOOD located at marker #248 near Barnes Bridge

Minnie Elizabeth married John William PACE on September 28, 1891. They had three children; Emma Adeline (b. 1891), Marie, and Harold. Confusion resulted because Minnie had to give her children up to an orphanage. John died in 1896. Minnie & the kids moved in with Thomas & Sarah. Both Thomas & Sarah died in 1899, leaving Minnie destitute. She gave her kids up and spent most of her life as a live-in domestic to well-to-do people. She eventually did marry again to a man named Cross (which is why she's known in my family as "Grandma Cross"). Emma Adeline married Guy Astor Bowman. Her line led to

Martha Sue Pigg who read the Elliott web page and made the connection in 2001.

The history of the 51ˢᵗ OVI was included in the History of Coshocton County, Ohio, published by A. A. GRAHM & CO., Newark Ohio, 1881, pp., 337–344.
Elliott, Thomas, U.S. Military Service Record, 1861–1865. Veterans Records, National Archives, Washington, D.C.

Date: Tue, 28 Nov 2000 12: 59: 58–0600 Marella wrote Hi! I'm so excited. I happened to surf into your site today on Nathan Elliott's family tree. I'd been hunting for Thomas Elliott (brother of Nathan relatives and ancestors for a while, but hadn't had any luck. And then, poof! there's a bunch of info right in front of me. I'd found several places that confirmed Thomas' marriage to Sarah Dawson, and his death date, but that was it (except for a rumor that his father was from Ireland). Anyway, it REALLY made my day!
Source: Martha Kneib.

28. Record of the Family as given by Mary Finlay Hester, Jan. 30, 1903

MARY FINLAY HESTER (1824–1904) In the spring of 1834, James and John Elliott took two teams of horses and wagons to Jefferson County to bring the Finlay families to Holmes County. The family lived for a year in the house of his father's cousin, James Elliott. George Finlay was his godfather at his baptism. During July of that summer Alice married John Graham, July 7, 1834. Mary told the story of the Finlay family in America throughout her lifetime.

Hester, Mary Finlay, Record of the Finlay Family as given by Mary Finlay Hester, January, 30, 1903. Unpublished Report, Holmes County Library, Millersburg, OH.

29. Genealogy of the David and Alice Finlay Family

Rev. Joseph Villars Finley (1843–1908) wrote that our grandmother, Alice (Elliott) Finley (1790–1866) came to America from Donegal County, Ireland, with her parents, George Elliott and wife Isabella Blaine, in 1802 when she was 12 years of age. In 1847, Alice Finley and family moved to Holmes County, Ohio. During a large part of her married life Alice (Finley) Elliott made her home in Western Iowa, at Whiting. Joseph documented records of their family descendants throughout Ohio and other States.

Finley, J. V., Rev., Genealogy of the David and Alice Finley Family—1777–1924. Unpublished report, Holmes County Library, 10 West Jackson St., Millerburg, OH 44654, 1–20 pp.

30. Finlay Family in Ohio

Roger Finlay of Urbana, Ohio, found Fanny Blaine Elliott's grave in the Keene Methodist Cemetery when he went to photograph Finlay and Finley stones. In the Coshocton Public Library, Roger discovered the Blaine connection with our Elliott/Finley families. Several of his photos have Elliott stones in the background. He has five generations of the Finley line of descendants from Moses Blaine Finley (1.2.1.5) and Sarah Jane Moore, which included about fifty names added to the Blaine/Elliott/Finley. They still need to be checked for accuracy.

Date: Sat, 23 Dec 2000 00:14:20–0500 Email from: Roger Finlay

31. Saunders Family from England to Rhode Island to California

The name of Tobias Saunders first appears in the records of Taunton, Massachusetts in 1643 and is thought to have died in 1695, as his will was proved on the second of September in that year. Although he was a member of the first Seventh Day Baptist Church in America at Newport, his ancestor, Rev. Lawrence Saunders, was not known to have been a Sabbath-keeper. He was one of the Christian martyrs burned to death outside the city of Coventry, England, on Sabbath Day, February 9, 1555.

Tobias Saunders was a soldier of the King in old England and at one time was one of the King's Life Guards. He was made a freeman in Newport in 1655 and on September 9, 1661, received a quarter of a share in the division of the land at Misquamicut as Westerly was then called. Several generations of Saunders were sailors of New England's best ships of the sea.

The Saunders family line continues with Nathan Saunders' (1750–1812) daughter, Matilda (1791–1862), who married Asa Crandall (1778–1849) in 1808/1809 in Charlestown, Washington County, Rhode Island. Nathan Saunders was a sea captain and lost at sea with his crew. Both Benjamin and his son Daniel had a son named Nathan. They lived in the heart of a traditional Yankee community where the men went to sea in wooden ships fishing for cod, whales and other sea food off the Grand Banks of New England.

Dorothy Ross Williams Unkrick (1910–?) and her mother Esther Bonnett Williams (1882–1942) collected basic genealogy for Saunders cousins in Iowa. A number of Saunders families moved to California during the late 19th Century. Some kept in touch with their relatives in Iowa, but others lost connections as relatives died.

Descendant Scott Wardlow found the Nathan Saunders Elliott web site on the Internet through a web page. Scott Howard Wardlow sent a set of Saunders quarterly from Lompoc, California. The story in the quarterly detailed the movement of several Saunders families from Iowa/Missouri to Lompoc, California. Scott got a kick out of the saloon story that was in the quarterly about James Saunders, his 3xgreat-grandfather, and the other men pulling down the saloon. At the beginning of the 20th Century, over one hundred Saunders people lived in Lompoc, California.

Lompoc Legacy, Lompoc Valley Historical Society, Inc., Quarterly Bulletin, Copy No 16, 77 was a dry year, winter, 1977.
Lompoc Legacy, Lompoc Valley Historical Society, Inc., Quarterly Bulletin, Copy No 17, and the Town Grew, Spring, 1978.
Nathan Saunders family records were gather by Dorothy Ross Williams Unkrick (1910–), from information obtained from family members over a period of years with the help of her mother Esther Bonnett Williams (1882–1942).

32. Isgrigg Family from England to Kentucky, Illinois and Missouri

William Isgrigg (1680–1755) was born and died in England. His grandson William Isgrigg III (1721–1780) was also born in England, but transported to Maryland for stealing silver buckles from his "master", married and died in Baltimore. His son, Michael Nicholson Isgrigg (1751–1832) served with a Maryland Co. in the Revolutionary War and afterwards his family moved west. One of his sons, Henry Isgrigg (1770?–1850?) served in the War of 1812 and later settled in South Missouri. His son, Jesse T. (1808–1891), born in Kentucky, was a veteran of the Black Hawk War, the Mexican War and the American Civil War. Jesse T. lived in Franklin Co., Missouri before moving to Holt County, Missouri in 1850. During the Civil War, he served with the 14th Kansas Cavalry, Co. K, through Missouri, Kansas, Arkansas, Indian Territory and Texas (1864–1865). He is buried in a private cemetery near Mound City, Missouri. His daughter, Sarah Isgrigg married William T. Redmon.

Janet Elliott Ewart visited family cousins in Missouri, Kansas, Iowa, Kentucky and Nebraska over a thirty-year period. She collected basic genealogy, name, birthday, marriage date and place, spouse names as well as their previous names and marriages, names of children, birth and death dates as well as Census information for many cousins.

HCMP and Bible Record—1891—Caton note: Jesse Isgrigg served as Justice of the peace in Holt Co., MO, for over 40 years. He took part in three wars—Black Hawk, Mexican and Civil Wars.

Weber, Yvonne J.G., The Isgrig/Isgrigg Family History, Gateway Press, Incl., Baltimore, MD, 1992, pp. 194.

Vass, Carol Glass, 14610 SE 266th St, Kent, WA, USA, 98042–8110, in an email: Date: Sun, 3 Jan 1999 20:05:44 EST To: exe1@psu.edu, regarding: Isgrigg.

Weber, Yvonne J. G., The Isgrig/Isgrigg Family History, Gateway Press, Inc., Baltimore, MD, 1992. 847 pages.

33. Carlton Family from England to New England and West

The known Carlton family line begins in England with Thomas Culton, his father???John Carleton and wife Ellen Strickland, their son Walter (1582–1623) and wife, Jane Gibbon, their son Edward (1610–1649) and wife Ellen Newton who brought their four children to Rowley, Massachusetts in 1639.

Their first child, John was born in England, settled in Haverhill, Massachusetts, married Hannah Jewett and fathered four sons, John, Jr., Joseph, Edward and Thomas. Edward (1665–1708) married Elizabeth Kimball and had a family of nine children. Edward, Jr. married Hanna C. Kimball, fathered six children, son John married Lydia Ladd and moved his family of ten children to Tollard County, Connecticut. Their oldest son, Kimball (1744–1832) had two families. He abandoned Sarah Kingsburg and seven children after the Revolution in which he served as a Continental Soldier at the Battle of Bennington. He faked his death and traveled south to Virginia and Kentucky where he married Elizabeth Spillman, moved west to Hardin County, Kentucky and fathered seven more children. Among his descendants, Eda Carlton (1803–1877) became the second wife of George W. Redmon (Redman) and bore five children including William T. Redmon.

Eda12 Carlton (Kimball11, John10, Edward9, Edward8 Carleton, John7, Edward6, Walter5, John4, Thomas3, John2, Thomas1 Culton) was born February 18, 1804 in Mercer County, Kentucky, USA, and died February 02, 1877. She married George Redman March 13, 1822

Children of Eda Carlton and George Redman are:
+94 i. Madison13 Redman, born October 06, 1822; died Unknown.
+95 ii. William T. Redman, born October 26, 1824; died March 06, 1906.
+96 iii. Madlinda Redman, born January 25, 1827; died Unknown.
+97 iv. Lewis Wayne Redman, born March 19, 1829 in Cole County, MO, USA; died August 30, 1862
+98 v. Peter Granville Redman, born August 10, 1831 in Cole County, MO, USA; died July 18, 1905
+99 vi. Elizabeth Redman, born August 11, 1833 in Cole County, Missouri, USA; died Unknown.
+100 vii. Martha Redman, born March 31, 1836 in Cole County, Missouri, USA; died Unknown.
+101 viii. John F. Redman, born February 20, 1838 in Cole County, Missouri, USA; died Unknown.
+102 ix. Taner Redman, born June 1840 in Cole County, Missouri, USA; died Unknown.

Database of Carlton Family in America. internet address: http://www.flash.net/~rcarlton/
Carleton/Carlton Forebears, SLC Book 929.273, C193a, 1977. P. Louise G. Boulter, in an email to ESE dated Nov. 5, 1998.

Shockley, Charline Pennell. The Carlton Family of Hardin County, Kentucky and related Families of Buckner, Corliss, Davis, Goodrich, Hartley, Hazeline, Jewett, Kimball, Ladd, Merril, Overall, Purdy, Scott, Smithers, Spotford, Spillman, Woodman. Santa Cruz California: privately published, 1986.
The Carlton Family of Hardin County, Kentucky and Related Families of privately published. Santa Cruz, California, 1986.
World family Tree, Vol. 5, Ed. 1, Tree #0089. Page: Tree #0089, Bruderbund Software, Ilc., Novato, California, Release Date: August 22, 1996, Tree # 0089.

Probate records of Essex County MA. Estate of John Carlton of Haverhill. Vol. 2, p 152. The probate Records of Essex County printed from early Vital Records of Essex County, MA (CD-RM, Copyright @ 1998, Search ReSearch Publishing Corp, Wheatridge, CO 80033.

34. Redmon(d) Family line from Kentucky to Illinois to Missouri.

George Redmon is a common name among early settlers in Kentucky. Maybe they were named for the first President, George Washington. Several Redmon families moved from Hardin County, Kentucky to the edge of the open prairie in Eastern Illinois in Edgar County, Coles Co. Other George Redmon lines settled around Paris, Illinois, county seat of Edgar County. (Not clear about ties between Redmon family lines in Kentucky.)

Census information was used to track the movement of the Redmon family in Missouri, Illinois, Kentucky and North Carolina. The county seat of Edgar County, Paris, Illinois was an important source of family information. (Janet Elliott Ewart—9/18/94 & 6/14/98) Family connection to Redmon line in Paris, Illinois is not clear. Here's the current story:

Family of Eda & George Redmon Religious Marriage Date: 1 Nov 1821. Children: Madison, William T., Madlinda, Lewis Wayne, Peter Granville, Elizabeth, Martha, John F., and Taner
GEORGE REDMON
Birth Date: 1794 Birth Place: ROWAN COUNTY, N.C.
Death Date: 1849 or before? (Janet E. Ewart—9/18/94)
Spouse: Edith "EDA" CARLTON
Birth Date: 18 Feb1804 Birth Place: KY
Death Date: 2 Feb 1877 Death Place: Mattoon, Illinois
1850 Census, Edgar Co., IL: Madison, age 27, Lewis, age 26, PeterG., age 17, Martha, age 11,JohnT, age 9
Spouse Father: KIMBALL CARLTON (1744–1830)
Spouse Mother: Elizabeth Spillman (1769–1851)
Burial: EDGAR/COLE families (J. E. Ewart 9/18/94)
Marriage Date: 1823 Marriage Place: KY or IL
Children:Madison,WILLIAM T., Lewis Wayne, Peter Granville, Martha, John F, Tanner.
Other spouses: Mae STICKLER?

Janet Elliott Ewart, Blockton, IO, is a g-granddaughter of William T. Redmon and his second wife, Sarah Isgrigg. Janet collected Redmon, Carlton, Isgrigg and Spillman family information over a period of years by visiting, sharing stories and completing a genealogy record of individuals and their families.

Janet Elliott Ewart visited family cousins in Missouri, Kansas, Iowa, Kentucky and Nebraska over a thirty-year period. She collected basic genealogy, name, birthday, marriage date and place, spouse names as well as their previous names and marriages, names of children, birth and death dates as well as Census information for many cousins.

35. Madison Redmon, oldest child of George and Eda

In July 2001, Celinda Kleinbeck, descendant of Madison Redmon, (6 Oct 1822–27 May 1902) reported the story about her g-grandparents.

The 1850 Census for Illinois places Eda with her children including Madison, who was twenty-seven years of age at the time. Madison went North after 1850 to Grant, Wisconsin, married and moved to southeast Kansas. The town of Humboldt, Kansas lies near Pittsburg, in the southeast part of Kansas. That's coal country, a place to get a hard job in the later part of the 19th century.

When Madison was still a child, his family moved from Kentucky to Coles County, Illinois, where he grew to manhood. In 1844, he became a citizen of the state of Wisconsin. He did live in Wisconsin in 1850 and that is where he met and married Olive Roxalain Crandall (4 Apr 1836–18 Sep 1902).

1.1 Madison A. Redmon b. 6 Oct 1822 Hardin, KY d. 27 May 1902 (GAR) Humboldt, KS married: 10 Sep 1852, Grant, WI spouse: Olive Roxalain Crandall b. 4 Apr 1836 Syracuse, NY d. 19 Sep 1902 Humboldt, KS. Parents: George Redmon b. 1794 Rowan, NC? d. 1835–1840 Edgar or Clark, IL married: 1 Nov 1821 Hardin, KY Edith "Eda" Carlton b. 18 Feb 1804 d. 2 Feb 1877. Grandparents: George Redmon b. 1748 Hardin, KY d. 1 Mar 1817 LaRue, KY married Abt. 3 June 1800 (alternate information says 1806) Delila Perciful b.16 Mar 1779 d. 6 Jun 1857 LaRue, Ky

1850 CENSUS Edgar Co., IL: Eda Redmon, Madison, age 27, Lewis, age 26, Peter G., age 17, Martha, age 11, John T., age 9

1880 Census: Madison lived on First Street, Humboldt, KS, located in the Southeast corner of Kansas. Major Industry: Coal Mining.
Military Record: WIS 12th Infantry.Co. K., Wisconsin Voluntary Infantry, Union, Dept. of Ks. Vicksburg Post 12, Rank In Private, Rank Out Private. Military Records—SC 106–018.

36. William T. Redmon Family Line in Kentucky, Illinois and Missouri

WILLIAM T. REDMON (26 Oct 1824–6 Mar 1906) farmed in the Missouri Valley near Craig, Missouri, Holt County. William T. Redmon married three times, Amelia L. Cunningham, Sarah Isgrigg, and Mary Edda Wilson McElhaney and fathered six children. He served with the 9th Missouri State Guard (1864–65) leaving his family to join his company in pursuit of Bill Anderson on the north side of the Missouri River. William T. was severely injured and crippled for life while riding hard across a creek on horseback. (Source: Janet Elliott Ewart—9/18/94)

1.2 WILLIAM T. REDMON*
Birth Date: Oct. 26, 1824 Birth Place: HARDIN COUNTY, KENTUCKY
Death Date: Mar 6, 1906 Death Place: Wadsworth, LEAVENWORTH, KS
Burial Place: NATIONAL CEMETERY, LEAVENWORTH, KS
Occupation: Farmer, served Civil War (Union, 9TH MISSOURI S.M. CAV
Education: Edgar Co., IL

1st wife Amerial; Children: Ann E. (1849–1925), Elvis Granville (1853–1914), John Colman (1856–1925) and Mary E. (1858–?)
Amerial L. Cunningham married William T. Redmon on 26 August 1848 in Edgar Co. IL. She was born in Mercer Co., KY. The family moved to Holt Co., MO shortly before the Civil War. Amerial died in 1862.

2nd wife Sarah Isgrigg Children: Ardella (1863–1916), Eda Virginia (1866–?)
Sarah Isgrigg married William T. Redmon, 12 October 1862 in Holt Co., Missouri. She was born in Franklin Co., Missouri and died 28 May 1887 near Craig, Missouri. She was buried in the Canton Family Cemetery, Mound City, Missouri.

Eva Redmon was living in St. Joseph, Missouri, at the time of Ardella's death. Her married name, Eva Burke appeared on Nathan Elliott's application for veteran's disability. She had a daughter named Virginia who married—Anderson who was in real estate in Kansas City, who died and was buried in Maryville, Missouri. A son, John Burke (–1983) married Nettie Mae Oliver (1899–1994) and had two children: a son, Kenneth Burke Pendergras and daughter, Rae who married a man named—Arnold living in Maple Hill, Kansas. Another son, Henry was living in Boise, Idaho. No other information.

William T. served in the Union Missouri Calvary, SM, from Feb. 1864 to May 1865. The 9th Missouri Cavalry State Militia served in the Department of Missouri during its entire career. The Regiment was attached to the Rolla District from Feb. 1862 through Feb. 1863 and the District of Northern Missouri Feb. 1863 through July 1865. Most actions took place on the north side of the Missouri River in the central and western parts of the state. The Regiment was formed by detachments between February 12, 1862 and finally reached full strength on September 30, 1863.

The Regiment was casually called by the name of its current commanding officer, i.e. Daniel M. Draper's Cavalry. The 9th participated in a variety of small skirmishes and minor actions beginning with Memphis, Missouri, on July 11, 1862. Final muster occurred in St. Joseph, Missouri on July 13, 1865. The Regiment lost during service two officers and twenty-nine enlisted men killed or mortally wounded and one officer and seventy-six enlisted men died of disease. Total casualties were one hundred eight.

May 18, 1865—Private Wm. T. Redman was mustered out of military service in St. Louis, MO.
August 10, 1866—Eda Virginia Redmon was born in Holt County, MO.
March 3, 1884—William T. Redmon (age 60) applied for an invalid pension.
Dec. 20, 1885—Ardella Redmon (age 22) married Nathan Elliott (age 44) in Craig.
Winter, 1886—Sarah Isgrigg Redmon (age 46) died in Holt County, MO.
September 6, 1888—William Redmon (age 64) married Mary E. McElhaney (age 44) in Holt Co., MO. by Jas. Anderson, minister.

December 23, 1895—In case number 314627, William T. Redmon (age 71) was pensioned under the Act of June 27, 1890. He received $12.00 per month veteran benefit for injuries due to disease of left varicocele (swollen veins in the spermatic cord) and disease of rectum and left hip.

March 21, 1905—William Redmon (age 81) was admitted to Wadsworth Veterans Hospital. He suffered from mitral insufficiency, blindness of the left eye, incontinence of urine, inguinal hernia; also weakness of mind due to senility. He had no memory of recent events, but said he would like to take care of himself, but could not think things out.

According to C.C. Cunningham, a life long acquaintance in Holt County, William T. Redmon was married three times. First, he married Amerial Cunningham, Cunningham's sister, who died in 1862. William Redmon afterwards married a woman by the name of Isgrig who died in 1886 or 1887. Afterwards he married Mary E. McElhaney (Aug 1, 1854–November 21, 1936). Mary Ella divorced Green McElhaney (January 12, 1886) who died prior to her marriage to William Redmon (September 6, 1888).

March 6, 1906—William Redmon (age 82) suffered a cerebral hemorrhage just preceding his death at 4:35 a.m. He was buried in Wadsworth National Cemetery, Section 21, row 2, grave #2912.

July 18, 1929—Mrs. Mary E. Redmon of Craig, MO was receiving a widow's pension of $30.00 a month. She was 75 years old in August. A letter from her Congressman supported a requested increased pension to $40.00 a month.

November 26, 1936—Mrs. Mary E. Redmon died of chronic microorganism failure and arteriosclerosis. She was a housekeeper for over 60 years and last worked in 1934. She was born in Metamora, Illinois in 1854. Her parents were Reed W. Wilson, born in Wayne Co, Indiana and Martha J. Brown, born in Virginia. She was buried in the IOOF Cemetery, Craig, Missouri.

1860 Census (Dallis township): Wm Redmon, age 36, Ky, America, age 33, MO, Ann, age 10, Elvis, age 7, John C., age 4, Mary E., age 2.
1870 Census (page 27): Wm Redmon, age 45, from Ky, Sarah, age 33, from MO, Ann, age 20, IL, Elvis, age 17, MO, John age14, MO, Ardella, age 7, MO, Eda Virginia, age 4, MO.
1880 Census (page 2): Wm Redmon, age 56, Ky, Sallie (Sarah), age 41, MO, Ardellia Lee, age 17, MO, Eda V., Age 12, MO, James Ballard, Hired Hand, Jesse W. Isgrigg, age 71, Ky.

Donna Lawson, Lebanon, Missouri is a g-g-granddaughter of Elvis Granville Redmon who was a son of William T. and his first wife, Amelia Cunningham Redmon. Donna visited Paris, Illinois, Dec. 1997, where she found George Redmon family information in the Historical Library. The information is located in the Davis Family History file and listed George's parents as George who married Nancy Bruce. The DAR list included George (father of Ledstone). Based on information in the DAR list, that George was too near our George's age to have been his father. Donna believes he was probably a cousin.

Donna located information that Bennett Redmon's son Joseph founded the town of Redmon, Illinois, a small community along the road west of Paris, Illinois. She also found that a George Redmon is buried in the Green Cemetery on the Steward farm south of Paris, Illinois. In a copy of probate records she found a note in a vertical file which, at the end, indicated the existence of Family Bible Records for a John Redman who died Jan., 1806 at Lexington, SC. He was a son of George Redman, born 24 Mar 1747, Frederick County, Virginia and died April 5, 1837, Edgar County, Illinois. This information was from Edythe Stephens, Paris, Illinois, 1981, or one of her children. The question is "Where is the Bible"?

In June 2001, Earl S. and Charles Earl Elliott, Jr. visited Paris, IL met in the Edgar County Genealogical Society Center with two direct George Redmon descendants. Gloria Mitchell is a descendant of Joseph Redmon. Linda Mabry is a direct descendant of Ledstone Redmon (Steve and Linda Mabry). They are both descendants of George Redmon. Together, they visited the private cemetery about two miles south of Paris, Illinois, the Revolutionary War Marker in the Center Square, the Methodist Church with a large Redmon Memorial Window, and had lunch at Westbrook Farm, which was originally built and owned by Smallwood (Bud) Redmon. (ESE took pictures and video of the trip.)

Dyer, Frederick H., A Compendium of the War of the Rebellion. Broadfoot Publishing Co., Morningside Press, 1994. pp. 1309.
Walter, John F., Capsule History, 9th Missouri Cavalry, SM, April 1993, Rev. Feb. 1996.
William T. Redmon, Company C, 9th Missouri Cavalry, SM (State Militia) buried in Wadsworth Cemetery (#21, Row 2912), Leavenworth, KS Source: Missouri State Historical Library, Springfield, MO

Lots of Redmon descendants live in Northwest Missouri, today. But, getting the right George Redmon would help focus our search. LaRue and Hardin KY are the same. Kentucky is the next place to visit!

References

Bauer, Dorothy June, daughter of Grace Elliott Miller, conversations and letters regarding family history, 1992–1996.

Boyd, Daniel D. & Augusta Crawford Boyd, One Hundred Years in America 1820–1920. Genealogy of the Family of Albert Boyd, Ireland. Unpublished booklet, 1920.

Duke, John K., History of the Fifty-Third Regiment Ohio Volunteer Infantry, during the War of the Rebellion, 1861 TO 1865. Bland Printing Co., Portsmith, Ohio, 1900.

Dyer, Frederick H., A Compendium of the War of the Rebellion. Broadfoot Publishing Co., Morningside Press, 1994. pp. 1309.

Elliott, Blanche, "Frances Blaine Elliott, honorable mention in Ohioana Library Essay Contest, Coshocton, Ohio,1941.

Elliott, Daniel G., U.S. Military Service Record, 1861–1865. Veterans Records, National Archives, Washington, D.C.

Elliott, Dorothy Talbert, wife of Ira Jr., conversations and letters regarding the Martha Malicent Yates Elliott family, 1994–1996.

Elliott, Earl S. Jr.,"Three Days at Shiloh". Unpublished manuscript, 53rd OVI during the Battle of Shiloh, 64 pp., 1994.

Elliott, Earl S., Jr. "Vicksburg to Chattanooga, Atlanta, Savannah and the Winter Carolinas March." Unpublished manuscript on the Campaigns of the 53rd OVI and the XV CORPS in the American Civil War, 1861–1865. 123 pp., 1996.

Elliott, Earl S., Jr. (Editor) wrote 500 to 1000 word essays about Elliott family members and their descendants. 1992, 1994, 1996, 1998.

Elliott, John Frizell "Lell" Elliott Jr., great grandson of James collected family history of James Elliott line of descendants. He visited Coshocton County several times during the 1970's, made maps of the Elliott Cemetery and Keene U.M. Cemetery and documented the Jame's generational line. John Frizell Elliott Jr. (Lell) gathered John Elliott/Fanny Blaine information concerning the descendants of their oldest son, James in the 1960's & 1970's.

Elliott, Hayward L. and daughter, Elaine Elliott, gathered family history, records and pictures that date to Daniel Gross Elliott, May,1998.

Elliott, Nathan S., U.S. Military Service Record and Veterans Benefits application 1861–1865, 1890, 1901, 1907, 1915, 1916.

Elliott, Thomas, U.S. Military Service Record, 1861–1865. Veterans Records, National Archives, Washington, D.C.
Elliott, Ardella Lee Redmon, wife of Nathan Elliott in a letter to Charley (her son), dated Sept. 14, 1914.

Elliott, Elizabeth C. Chamberlin, 1880–1968, wife of Earl Saunders Elliott Sr.(1887–1944).Unpublished notes, collected over 23 years.

Elliott, Elizabeth Catherine, "Bess" or "Lizzie", conversations and letters to Ruth Shipman dated April 9, 1956., a letter to Becky Stevens (age 4) dated Easter, 1958.

Elliott, Harold Earl, oldest son of Charles Metz Elliott, conversations and letters regarding the Nathan Elliott family.

Elliott, Harold Earl, oldest son of Charles Metz Elliott, in a letter dated February 19, 1991 and posted from 17134 Greenbay Ave., Lansing, Illinois 60438.

Elliott, Melvin and Doris, letters, conversations regarding James Elliott family line, 1992–1996.

Elliott, Ruth (daughter of Nathan & Ardella) in a letter to Charley Elliott, while he was away at school, dated March 24, 1913.

Elliott Reunions, 1990, 1992, 1994, 1996. Sugar Creek Church, Rushville, MO with families of 16 first cousins of the Children of Nathan Saunders Elliott.

Elliott, Thomas, youngest brother of Nathan Elliott, U.S. Military Service Record, 1861–1865. Veterans Records, National Archives, Washington, D.C.

Ewart, Janet Elliott, contacted cousins in Missouri, Kansas, Iowa, Kentucky and Nebraska over a 30 year period. She collected basic genealogy, name, birthday, marriage date and place, spouse names including Census information.

Finley, J. V., Rev., Genealogy of the David and Alice Finley Family—1777 to 1924. Unpublished report, Holmes County Library, 10 West Jackson St., Miller-burg, OH 44654 1–20 pp.

Finlay, Roger Descendant of Finlay family in Ohio. Finley line of descendants from Moses Blaine Finley (1.2.1.5) and Sarah Jane Moore, 2001.

Goodspeed, _. History of Missouri, 1889, including a History of Texas County.

Haselmayer, Louis A., Prof., Iowa Wesleyan College, The Presidents of Iowa Wesleyan College, 1967.

Harvey, Nancy Elliott descendant of Thomas Elliott and Nancy Nutt.

Hester, Mary Finlay, Record of the Finlay Family as given by Mary Finlay Hester, January, 30, 1903. Unpublished Report, Holmes County Library, Millersburg, Ohio.

Heiser, H. Arlan, gr-gr-grandson of "Blacksmith George Elliott" who lived on the next farm to Fanny Blaine Elliott in Holmes Co., OH. Received several letters from Arlan with significant Blaine, Elliott, Boyd and Finley family information, Fall, 1996. Address: 10594 Partridge Trail, Brecksville, OH 44141.

Hunt, W.E., Historical Collection of Coshocton County, Ohio, 1864–1876, Robert Clarke and Co, Printers, Cincinnati, Ohio, 1876, p. 208.

Inman, Benjamin P., grandson of Cora "LILLIE" Lillian Elliott, letters and telephone conversations, 1994–1996.

Isgrigg, Jesse, HCMP and Bible Record—1891—Caton note: Jesse Isgrigg served as Justice of the peace in Holt Co., MO, for over 40 years. He took part in three wars—Black Hawk, Mexican and Civil, pp. 194.

Kintner, E. P., Edward Kintner and Glada Snyder Ancestral Genealogy and Tour Guide, 1994. Published: 1314 Turnberry Ln., Maryville, TN 37801. Personal family history through eight generations that includes Mary (Marie) Elliott, oldest daughter of John/Fanny Blaine Elliott.

Kleinbeck, Celinda, reported the life and times of Madison Redmon.

Kneib, Martha, descendant of Thomas Elliott and Sarah Dawson.

Lawrence, Jay, A History of the Keene Churches, 1968, pp. 1–15 based on family records of Zelma Wheatcraft regarding the Elliott family and their settlement in Coshocton County in 1816 and participation in the establishment of the U.M. Church in Keene.

Lompoc Legacy, Lompoc Valley Historical Society, Inc., Quarterly Bulletin, Copy No 16, 77 was a dry year, Winter 1977.

Lompoc Legacy, Lompoc Valley Historical Society, Inc., Quarterly Bulletin, Copy No 17, and the Town Grew, Spring, 1978.

Norton, Ruth M., great granddaughter of George Elliott and historian at Roscoe Village, in a letter to Earl S. Elliott Jr., reported finding a letter (June 16th 1842) written by Samuel Elliott to his brother-in-law, Daniel Boyd (Athens County)., James Elliott to his brother-in-law, Daniel Boyd (Athens County)., Maryann Boyd to her mother and father, Jane Elliott Boyd & Daniel Boyd (Athens County)., Daniel Boyd (Athens County) to Nathan Elliott (53rd OVI) about the politics of the War, written near the end of the Civil War, 1865. Roscoe Village Foundation.

Official Roster of the Soldiers of the State of Ohio in the War of the Rebellion, 1861–1865. No. l. IV: 37th–53rd Regiments—Infantry, published by the Authority of the General Assembly, Werner PTG and MFG Co., 1887, 44 (673)

McCush, Helen Hope Elliott, daughter of Charles Metz Elliott, letters and conversations regarding family history, 1992–1996.

Miller, Carl, letters and conversations, regarding family history. 1992–1996.

Miller, Clarence & Luetta, letters and conversations, regarding family history, 1992–1996.

Redmon, William T., Company C, 9th Missouri Cavalry, SM (State Militia) buried in Wadsworth Cemetery (#21, Row 2912), Leavenworth, KS. Source: Missouri State Historical Library, Springfield, MO.

Richter, Edward, Jr., husband of Ardellia Shipman, letters and conversations regarding the life and times of his wife, 1994.

Roscoe Village Foundation, Letters from Samuel Elliott, George Elliott, and the Daniel Boyd family, 1842–1849–1965.

Shipman, Russell, son of Ruth Elliott Shipman, conversations and letters regarding family history, 1992–1996.

Stevens, Virginia, daughter of Ruth Elliott Shipman. Letters and conversations, 1992–1996. Plus, letter dated September 20, 1990, and posted from 3388 Orchard Drive, Bountiful, Utah 84010. Copies of notes and pictures collected by her mother over the years.

Unkrick, Dorthy Ross Williams, Nathan Saunders family records gathered information obtained from family members over a period of years with the help of her mother Esther Bonnett Williams (1882–1942).

Walter, John F., Capsule History, 9th Missouri Cavalry, SM, April, 1993, Rev. Feb. 1996.

Walker, ___. History of Athens County, 1869, pp. 457. Information on Kos Elliott was from "The History of Jasper County, MO" (L.L. Thompson, 5/27/97)

Wardlow, Scott W. collected Saunders Family History in the West. He shared a set of Saunders quarterlies from Lompoc, CA and other Saunders family history. 1998.

—Wilson County Citizen and Guilford Citizen, published April 21, 1870, Guilford, Kansas until Vol. 1: 27, then moved to Neodasha, Kansas, May 28, 1870 and August 20, 1870.

—Official Roster of the Soldiers of the State of Ohio in the War of the Rebellion, 1861–1865. No. l. IV: 37th–53rd Regiments—Infantry, published by the Authority of the General Assembly, Werner PTG and MFG Co., 1887, 44 (673)

Reference Notes

Reference Note 7
Duke, John K., History of the Fifty-Third Regiment Ohio Volunteer Infantry, during the War of the Rebellion, 1861 TO 1865. Bland Printing Co., Portsmith, Ohio, 1900.

Reference Note 8
Elliott, Ardella Lee Redmon, wife of Nathan Elliott in a letter to Charley (her son), dated Sept. 14, 1914.

Reference Note 12
McGill, P.J., History of the Parish of Ardara.
Tells the story of the Parish from early ages to the 20th century. Dr. Charles Elliott & Kilclooney, Spanish Armada Dister of Kiltoorish, how the "Mere" Irish" were dispersed. The Rebels of 1641 in Ardara. Donegal Clans and Ulster Irish. The Penal Laws., Irish tweed and the woolen trade and emigration from South Donegal. 1970

Reference Note 13
Athens County Marriages 1805–1865, Vol. 1 np

Reference Note 14
Boyd, Daniel D. & Augusta C., One Hundred Years in America, 1820–1920, in custody of personal library of Marjorie Ward, Hilliard, Ohio, pg 12, and Jeannette Gaskell Chevervenka, Boyd-Elliott-Eichhorn Connection, in custody of personal library of Nancy Leinweber, Euclid, OH, pg 532 & 69–71.

Reference Note 15
Leinweber, Nancy. Jeannette Gaskell Chervenka, Boyd-Ellliott-Eichhor Connection, in custody of her personal library, Euclid, OH, pg 69.

Reference Note 21
Elliott, Charles H.,Winfield Public Library. Biographical Sketches, Leading Citizens of Cowley Co.,1901. From the Winfield Public Library, Winfield, KS

Reference Note 28
Elliott, Earl S. Jr."Three Days at Shiloh". Unpublished manuscript on the 53rd OVI at the Battle of Shiloh, 64 pp., 1994.

Reference Note 29
Elliott, Earl S., Jr. "Vicksburg to Chattanooga, Atlanta, Savannah and the Winter Carolinas March." Unpublished manuscript on the Campaigns of the 53rd OVI and the XV CORPS in the American Civil War, 1861–1865. 123 pp., 1996.

Reference Note 36
Elliott, Nathan S., U.S. Military Service Record and Veterans Benefits application 1861–1865, 1890, 1901, 1907, 1915, 1916.

Reference Note 37
Elliott, Ruth (daughter of Nathan & Ardella) in a letter to Charley Elliott, while he was away at school, dated March 24, 1913.

Reference Note 39
Elliott, Thomas, youngest brother of Nathan Elliott, U.S. Military Service Record, 1861–1865. Veterans Records, National Archives, Washington, D.C.

Reference Note 40
Hunt, W.E., Historical Collection of Coshocton County, Ohio, 1864–1876, Robert Clarke and Co., Printers, Cincinnati, Ohio, 1876, p. 208.

Reference Note 42
Lawrence, Jay, A History of the Keene Churches, 1968, pp. 1–15. based on family records of Zelma Wheatcraft regarding the Elliott family and their settlement in Coshocton County in 1816 and participation in the establishment of the U.M. Church in Keene.

Reference Note 50
—Official Roster of the Soldiers of the State of Ohio in the War of the Rebellion, 1861–1865. No. l. IV: 37th–53rd Regiments—Infantry, published by the Authority of the General Assembly, Werner PTG and MFG Co., 1887, 44 (673)

Reference Note 51
—Wilson County Citizen and Guilford Citizen, published April 21, 1870, Guilford, Kansas until Vol. 1: 27, then moved to Neodasha, Kansas, May 28, 1870 and August 20, 1870.

Reference Note 55
AVE:Reunion 6–2 Folder:***Master Reunion 3/21/99:
"Several Ancestral Lines of James P. Refrew and His Wife, Ella Black" by James P. Renfrew, Alva OK, Alva Record Print, Alva OK, age 70. from Karen Lee (Hill) Walker, 1281 NW Bus 36 Hwy Hamilton, MO 64644. Tel: (816) 538–2350

0-595-30584-9